I0460860

TONE OF THE MUNAFIQ

By Gregory Heary

This book is about the indicators of the Munafiq/hypocrite. A Munafiq/hypocrite is one who openly professes Islam but believes in other than Islam. Historically they would rarely express their disbelief by tongue or limb but in modern times it has become common for the deviants among the sects to proclaim their kufr openly but in the guise of Islam. Therefore the Munafiq/hypocrite is the most dangerous enemy of Islam and the Muslims because of its camouflage and manipulative cunning two-facedness with their ability to mislead the Muslims while they think they are rightly guided. Jihad against the Munafiq by the heart, dua, pen, tongue and limbs is the peak of the peak of Islam. Unfortunately as Allah says in 4:88 what means: *What is [the matter] with you [that you are] two groups concerning the hypocrites, while Allah has made them fall back [into error and disbelief] for what they earned. Do you wish to guide those whom Allah has sent astray? And he whom Allah sends astray - never will you find for him a way [of guidance].* the Ummah today has varying opinions and treatments regarding the worst of the worst of creation. Yet as Allah commanded his prophet in 9:73 and 66:9 *O Prophet, strive against the disbelievers and the hypocrites and be harsh upon them. And their refuge is Hell, and wretched is the destination.* it will always be an obligation to strive hard against the munafiqeen until the day of resurrection whether lightly equipped or heavily equipped. So it is in that spirit that this book is composed since dua, while the most powerful weapon against the munafiq, is not enough to discharge the duty of striving for those who have further capabilities. The trouble most Muslims have today is

3

not in coming to the correct conclusion about the danger of the Munafiq and the obligation to strive against them, but it is simple identification. Hence this identification manual is to expose and warn of the danger of the Munafiqeen; inshallah with heed being taken by the reader before more damage is done to the blessed Ummah of the prophets. Always remember when identifying a Munafiq if its not by their actions, or statements then *you will surely know them by the tone of [their] speech.* (47:30) and also their silence in some instances can be included in "the tone of their speech" as an identification method. This book will proceed with the Quranic citations regarding the Munafiqeen accompanied by some of the Tafsir of those ayat by ibn kathir followed by hadith and a list of modern-day qualities of munafiqeen compiled by the Mindoro Islamic Research Center which I have edited. May the changer of hearts, remove such qualities from us, our offspring, families, friends and nation.

Quranic citations with Tafsir about hypocrites

2:8-20

And of mankind, there are some (hypocrites) who say: "We believe in Allâh and the Last Day" while in fact they believe not. (8) They (think to) deceive Allâh and those who believe, while they only deceive themselves, and perceive (it) not! (9) In their hearts is a disease (of doubt and hypocrisy) and Allâh has increased their disease. A painful torment is theirs because they used to tell lies. (10) And when it is said to them: "Make not mischief on the earth," they say: "We are only peacemakers." (11) Verily! They are the ones who make mischief, but they perceive not. (12) And when it is said to them (hypocrites): "Believe as the people (followers of Muhammad, Al-Ansâr and Al-Muhajirûn) have believed," they say: "Shall we believe as the fools have believed?" Verily, they are the fools, but they know not (13) And when they meet those who believe, they say: "We believe," but when they are alone with their Shayâtin (devils - polytheists, hypocrites), they say: "Truly, we are with you; verily, we were but mocking." (14) Allâh mocks at them and gives them increase in their wrong-doings to wander blindly. (15) These are they who have purchased error for guidance, so their commerce was profitless. And they were not guided. (16) Their likeness is as the likeness of one who kindled a fire; then, when it lighted all around him, Allâh took away their light and left them in darkness. (So) they could not see. (17) They are deaf, dumb, and blind, so they return not (to the Right Path). (18) Or like a rainstorm from the sky, wherein is darkness, thunder, and lightning. They thrust their fingers in their ears to keep out the stunning thunderclap for fear of death. But Allâh ever encompasses the disbelievers (i.e. Allâh will gather them all together). (19) The lightning almost snatches away their sight, whenever it flashes for them, they walk therein, and when darkness covers them, they stand still. And if Allâh willed, He could have taken away their hearing and their sight. Certainly, Allâh has power over all things.

The hypocrites show belief outwardly while concealing disbelief. They think that by doing this, they will mislead Allah, or that the statements they utter will help them with Allah, and this is an indication of their total ignorance. They think that such behavior will deceive Allah, just as it might deceive some of the believers. *And of mankind, there are some who say: "We believe in Allah and the Last Day'' while in fact they believe not. They try to deceive Allah and those who believe, while they only deceive themselves, and perceive (it) not!* "This is the description of a hypocrite. He is devious, he says the truth with his tongue and defies it with his heart and deeds. He wakes up in a condition other than the one he goes to sleep in, and goes to sleep in a different condition than the one he wakes up in. He changes his mind just like a ship that moves about whenever a wind blows.'' As-Suddi narrated from Abu Malik and (also) from Abu Salih, from Ibn `Abbas, and (also) Murrah Al-Hamdani from Ibn Mas`ud and other Companions that this Ayah,

In their hearts is a disease means, `doubt', and, *And Allah has increased their disease* also means `doubt'. Mujahid,

`Ikrimah, Al-Hasan Al-Basri, Abu Al-`Aliyah, Ar-Rabi` bin Anas and Qatadah also said similarly.

Allah said next, *Because they used to tell lies.* The hypocrites have two characteristics, they lie and they deny the Unseen. The scholars who stated that the Prophet knew the hypocrites of his time have only the Hadith of Hudhayfah bin Al-Yaman as evidence. In it the Prophet gave him the names of fourteen hypocrites during the battle of Tabuk. These hypocrites plotted to assassinate the Prophet during the night on a hill in that area. They planned to excite the Prophet's camel, so that she would throw him down the hill. Allah informed the Prophet about their plot, and the Prophet told Hudhayfah their names. As for the other hypocrites, Allah said about them,

And among the bedouins around you, some are hypocrites, and so are some among the people of Al-Madinah who persist in hypocrisy; you (O Muhammad) know them not, We know them (9:101), and, If the hypocrites, and those in whose hearts is a disease, and those who spread false news among the people in Al-Madinah do not cease, We shall certainly let you overpower them, then they will not be able to stay in it as your neighbors but a little while. Accursed, they shall be seized wherever found, and killed with a (terrible) slaughter (33:60-61).

These Ayat prove that the Prophet was not informed about each and everyone among the hypocrites of his time. Rather, the Prophet was only informed about their characteristics, and he used to assume that some people possessed these characteristics. Similarly, Allah said,

Had We willed, We could have shown them to you, and you should have known them by their marks; but surely, you will know them by the tone of their speech! (47:30).

The most notorious hypocrite at that time was `Abdullah bin Ubayy bin Salul; Zayd bin Arqam - the Companion - gave truthful testimony to that effect.  In addition, `Umar bin Al-Khattab once mentioned the matter of Ibn Salul to the Prophet , who said,

I would not like the Arabs to say to each other that Muhammad is killing his Companions.

Yet, when Ibn Salul died, the Prophet performed the funeral prayer for him and attended his funeral just as he used to do with other Muslims. It was recorded in the Sahih that the Prophet said,

I was given the choice (to pray for him or not), so I chose.

In another narration, the Prophet said,

If I knew that by asking (Allah to forgive Ibn Salul) more than seventy times that He would forgive him, then I would do that.

In his Tafsir, As-Suddi said that Ibn `Abbas and Ibn Mas`ud commented,

And when it is said to them: "Do not make mischief on the earth," *they say: "We are only peacemakers.'' "They are the hypocrites.*

As for, "*Do not make mischief on the earth*", that is disbelief and acts of disobedience." Abu Ja`far said that Ar-Rabi` bin Anas said that Abu Al-`Aliyah said that Allah's statement,

And when it is said to them: "Do not make mischief on the earth,", means, "Do not commit acts of disobedience on the earth. Their mischief is disobeying Allah, because whoever disobeys Allah on the earth, or commands that Allah be disobeyed, he has committed mischief on the earth. Peace on both the earth and in the heavens is ensured (and earned) through obedience (to Allah)." Ar-Rabi` bin Anas and Qatadah said similarly. Ibn Jarir said, "The hypocrites commit mischief on earth by disobeying their Lord on it and continuing in the prohibited acts. They also abandon what Allah made obligatory and doubt His religion, even though He does not accept a deed from anyone except with faith in His religion and certainty of its truth. The hypocrites also lie to the believers by saying contrary to the doubt and hesitation their hearts harbor. They give as much aid as they can, against Allah's loyal friends, and support those who deny Allah, His Books and His Messengers. This is how the hypocrites commit mischief on earth, while thinking that they are doing righteous work on earth."

Since the outward appearance of the hypocrite displays belief, he confuses the true believers. Hence, the deceitful behavior of the hypocrites is an act of mischief, because they deceive the believers by claiming what they do not believe in, and because they give support and loyalty to the disbelievers against the believers.

And when it is said to them: "*Do not make mischief on the earth,*" *they say: "We are only peacemakers.*" meaning, "We seek to be friends with both parties, the believers and the disbelievers, and to have peace with both parties." Similarly, Muhammad bin Ishaq reported that Ibn `Abbas said,

And when it is said to them: "Do not make mischief on the earth," *they say: "We are only peacemakers.*" means, "We seek to make amends between the believers and the People of the Book. "

Allah said that if the hypocrites are told,

"*Believe as the people believe,*", meaning, `Believe just as the believers believe in Allah, His angels, His Books, His Messengers, Resurrection after death, Paradise and Hellfire, etc. And obey Allah and His Messenger by heeding the commandments and avoiding the prohibitions.' Yet the hypocrites answer by saying, "*Shall we believe as the fools have believed*" they meant (may Allah curse the hypocrites) the Companions of the Messenger of Allah . This is the same Tafsir given by Abu Al-`Aliyah and As-Suddi in his Tafsir, with a chain of narration to Ibn `Abbas, Ibn Mas`ud and other Companions. This is also the Tafsir of Ar-Rabi` bin Anas and `Abdur-Rahman bin Zayd bin Aslam. The hypocrites said, "Us and them having the same status, following the same path, while they are fools!" `The fool' is the ignorant, simple-minded person who has little knowledge in areas of benefit and harm. This is why, according to the majority of the scholars, Allah used the term foolish to include children, when He said,

And do not give your property, which Allah has made a means of support for you, to the foolish (4:5).

Allah answered the hypocrites in all of these instances. For instance, Allah said here, *Verily, they are the fools.* Allah thus affirmed that the hypocrites are indeed the fools, yet, *But they know not.* Since they are so thoroughly ignorant, the hypocrites are unaware of their degree of deviation and ignorance. Such is more dangerous, a severer case of blindness, and further from the truth than one who is aware.

Allah said that when the hypocrites meet the believers, they proclaim their faith and pretend to be believers, loyalists and friends. They do this to misdirect, mislead and deceive the believers. The hypocrites also want to have a share of the benefits and gains that the believers might possibly acquire.

But when they are alone with their Shayatin, meaning, if they are alone with their devils, such as their leaders and masters among the rabbis of the Jews, hypocrites and idolators.

Ibn Jarir said, "The devils of every creation are the mischievous among them. There are both human devils and Jinn devils. Allah said, *Verily, we were but mocking*, meaning, we only mock people (the believers) and deceive them." Ad-Dahhak said that Ibn `Abbas said that the Ayah, *Verily, we were but mocking*, means, "We (meaning the hypocrites) were mocking the Companions of Muhammad." Also, Ar-Rabi` bin Anas and Qatadah said similarly. Allah's statement, *Allah mocks at them and leaves them increasing in their deviation to wander blindly* answers the hypocrites and punishes them.

Allah stated that He will punish the hypocrites for their mockery, using the same terms to describe both the deed and its punishment, although the meaning is different. Similarly, Allah said, *The recompense for an offense is an offense equal to it; but whoever forgives and makes reconciliation, his reward is with Allah* (42:40), and, *Then whoever transgresses (the prohibition) against you, transgress likewise against him* (2:194).

The first act is an act of injustice, while the second act is an act of justice. So both actions carry the same name, while being different in reality. This is how the scholars explain deceit, cunning and mocking when attributed to Allah in the Qur'an. Surely, Allah exacts revenge for certain evil acts with a punishment that is similar in nature to the act itself. We should affirm here that Allah does not do these things out of joyful play, according to the consensus of the scholars, but as a just form of punishment for certain evil acts.

Allah said, *Allah mocks at them and leaves them increasing in their deviation to wander blindly.* As-Suddi reported that Ibn `Abbas, Ibn Mas`ud and several other Companions of the Messenger of Allah said that, *and leaves them increasing* means, He gives them respite. Also, Mujahid said, "He (causes their deviation) to increase." Allah said; *Do they think that by the wealth and the children with which We augment them. (That) We hasten to give them with good things. Nay, but they perceive not.* (23:55-56). Ibn Jarir commented, "The correct meaning of this Ayah is `We give them increase from the view of giving them respite and leaving them in their deviation and rebellion.' Also, Ibn Jarir said that the term

`Amah, in the Ayah means, `deviation'. He also said about Allah's statement, *in their deviation to wander*, "In the misguidance and disbelief that has encompassed them, causing them to be confused and unable to find a way out of it. This is because Allah has stamped their hearts, sealed them, and blinded their vision. Therefore, they do not recognize guidance or find the way out of their deviation."

In his Tafsir, As-Suddi reported that Ibn `Abbas and Ibn Mas`ud commented on; *These are they who have purchased error with guidance* saying it means, "They pursued misguidance and abandoned guidance. " Mujahid said, "They believed and then disbelieved," while Qatadah said, "They preferred deviation to guidance." In summary, the hypocrites deviate from the true guidance and prefer misguidance, substituting wickedness in place of righteousness. This meaning explains Allah's statement, *These are they who have purchased error with guidance*, meaning, they exchanged guidance to buy misguidance. This meaning includes those who first believed, then later disbelieved, whom Allah described, *That is because they believed, and then disbelieved; therefore their hearts are sealed* (63:3). The Ayah also includes those who preferred deviation over guidance. The hypocrites fall into several categories. This is why Allah said, *So their commerce was profitless. And they were not guided*, meaning their trade did not succeed nor were they righteous or rightly guided throughout all this. In addition, Ibn Jarir narrated that Qatadah commented on the Ayah, *So their commerce was profitless. And they were not guided,* " By Allah! I have seen them leaving guidance for deviation, leaving the Jama`ah (the community of the believers) for the sects, leaving safety for fear, and the Sunnah for innovation." Ibn Abi Hatim also reported other similar statements.

Allah likened the hypocrites when they bought deviation with guidance, thus acquiring utter blindness, to the example of a person who started a fire. When the fire was lit, and illuminated the surrounding area, the person benefited from it and felt safe. Then the fire was suddenly extinguished. Therefore, total darkness covered this person, and he became unable to see anything or find his way out of it. Further, this person could not hear or speak and became so blind that even if there were light, he would not be able to see. This is why he cannot return to the state that he was in before this happened to him. Such is the case with the hypocrites who preferred misguidance over guidance, deviation over righteousness. This parable indicates that the hypocrites first believed, then disbelieved, just as Allah stated in other parts of the Qur'an.

When they suffer from doubt, confusion and disbelief, their hearts are, *Like a Sayyib,* meaning, "The rain", as Ibn Mas`ud, Ibn `Abbas, and several other Companions have confirmed as well as Abu Al-`Aliyah, Mujahid, Sa`id bin Jubayr, `Ata', Al-Hasan Al-Basri, Qatadah, `Atiyah Al-`Awfi, `Ata' Al-Khurasani, As-Suddi and Ar-Rabi` bin Anas. Ad-Dahhak said "It is the clouds." However, the most accepted opinion is that it means the rain that comes down during, *darkness,* meaning, here, the doubts, disbelief and hypocrisy. *thunder that shocks the hearts with fear.* The hypocrites are usually full of fear and anxiety, just as Allah described them, *They think that every cry is against them* (63: 4), and, *They swear by Allah that they are truly of you while they are not of you, but they are a people who are afraid. Should they find refuge, or caves, or a place of concealment, they would turn straightway thereto in a swift rush* (9:56-57).

The lightning, is in reference to the light of faith that is sometimes felt in the hearts of the hypocrites, *They thrust their fingers in their ears to keep out the stunning thunderclap for fear of death. But Allah ever encompasses the disbelievers,* meaning, their cautiousness does not benefit them because they are bound by Allah's all-encompassing will and decision. Allah then said, *The lightning almost snatches away their sight* meaning, because the lightning is strong itself, and because their comprehension is weak and does not allow them to embrace the faith. Also, `Ali bin Abi Talhah reported that Ibn `Abbas commented on the Ayah, *The lightning almost snatches away their sight,* "The Qur'an mentioned almost all of the secrets of the hypocrites." `Ali bin Abi Talhah also narrated that Ibn `Abbas said, *Whenever it flashes for them, they walk therein,* "Whenever the hypocrites acquire a share in the victories of Islam, they are content with this share. Whenever Islam suffers a calamity, they are ready to revert to disbelief." Also, Muhammad bin Ishaq reported that Ibn `Abbas said, *Whenever it flashes for them, they walk therein, and when darkness covers them, they stand still,* "They recognize the truth and speak about it. So their speech is upright, but

15

when they revert to disbelief, they again fall into confusion."
This was also said by Abu Al-`Aliyah, Al-Hasan Al-Basri,
Qatadah, Ar-Rabi` bin Anas and As-Suddi, who narrated it
from the Companions, and it is the most obvious and most
correct view, and Allah knows best.

Consequently, on the Day of Judgment, the believers will be
given a light according to the degree of their faith. Some of
them will gain light that illuminates over a distance of
several miles, some more, some less. Some people's light will
glow sometimes and be extinguished at other times. They
will, therefore, walk on the Sirat (the bridge over the Fire) in
the light, stopping when it is extinguished. Some people will
have no light at all, these are the hypocrites. There are
several types of people. There are the believers whom the
first four Ayat (2:2-5) in Surat Al-Baqarah describe. There are
the disbelievers who were described in the next two Ayat.
And there are two categories of hypocrites: the complete
hypocrites who were mentioned in the parable of the fire,
and the hesitant hypocrites, whose light of faith is
sometimes lit and sometimes extinguished. The parable of
the rain was revealed about this category, which is not as
evil as the first category. The believers are two categories,
the near ones and righteous. Also, the disbelievers are of two
types, advocates and followers. In addition, the hypocrites
are divided into two types, pure hypocrites and those who
have some hypocrisy in them. The Two Sahihs record
`Abdullah bin `Amr said the Prophet said, *Whoever has the
following three (characteristics) will be a pure hypocrite, and*

whoever has one of the following three characteristics will have one characteristic of hypocrisy, unless and until he gives it up. Whenever he speaks, he tells a lie. Whenever he makes a covenant, he proves treacherous. Whenever he is entrusted, he breaches the trust.

Imam Ahmad recorded Abu Sa`id saying that the Messenger of Allah said:

The hearts are four (types): polished as shiny as the radiating lamp, a sealed heart with a knot tied around its seal, a heart that is turned upside down and a wrapped heart. As for the polished heart, it is the heart of the believer and the lamp is the light of faith. The sealed heart is the heart of the disbeliever. The heart that is turned upside down is the heart of the pure hypocrite, because he had knowledge but denied it. As for the wrapped heart, it is a heart that contains belief and hypocrisy. The example of faith in this heart, is the example of the herb that is sustained by pure water. The example of hypocrisy in it, is the example of an ulcer that thrives on puss and blood. Whichever of the two substances has the upper hand, it will have the upper hand on that heart. This Hadith has a Jayid Hasan (good) chain of narration.

Allah said, *And if Allah willed, He would have taken away their hearing and their sight. Certainly, Allah has power over all things.* Muhammad bin Ishaq reported that Ibn `Abbas commented on Allah's statement, *And if Allah willed, He would have taken away their hearing and their sight*, "Because they abandoned the truth after they had knowledge in it." *Certainly, Allah has power over all things.* Ibn `Abbas said, "Allah is able to punish or pardon His servants as He wills." Ibn Jarir commented,

"Allah only described Himself with the ability to do everything in this Ayah as a warning to the hypocrites of His control over everything, and to inform them that His ability completely encompasses them and that He is able to take away their hearing and sight." Ibn Jarir and several other scholars of Tafsir stated that these two parables are about the same kind of hypocrite.

2:204-206

And of mankind there is he whose speech may please you, in this worldly life, and he calls Allâh to witness as to that which is in his heart, yet he is the most quarrelsome of the opponents. (204) And when he turns away, his effort in the land is to make mischief therein and to destroy the crops and the cattle, and Allâh likes not mischief. (205) And when it is said to him, "Fear Allâh", he is led by arrogance to (more) crime. So enough for him is Hell, and worst indeed is that place to rest!

As-Suddi said that these Ayat were revealed about Al-Akhnas bin Shariq Ath-Thaqafi who came to Allah's Messenger and announced his Islam although his heart concealed otherwise. Ibn `Abbas narrated that these Ayat were revealed about some of the hypocrites who criticized Khubayb and his companions who were killed during the Raji` incident. Thereafter, Allah sent down His condemnation of the hypocrites and His praise for Khubayb and his companions. It was also said that they refer to the hypocrites and the believers in general. This is the opinion of Qatadah, Mujahid, Ar-Rabi` bin Anas and several others, and it is correct.

Ibn Jarir related that Al-Qurazi said that Nawf Al-Bikali, who used to read (previous Divine) Books said, "I find the description of some members of this Ummah in the previously revealed Books of Allah: they (hypocrites) are people who use the religion to gain material benefit. Their tongues are sweeter than honey, but their hearts are more bitter than Sabir (a bitter plant, aloe). They show the people the appearance of sheep while their hearts hide the viciousness of wolves. Allah said, `They dare challenge Me, but they are deceived by Me. I swear by Myself that I will send a Fitnah (trial, calamity) on them that will make the wise man bewildered.' I contemplated about these statements and found them in the Qur'an describing the hypocrites: *And of mankind there is he whose speech may please you, in this worldly life, and he calls Allah to witness as to that which is in his heart,* this statement by Al-Qurazi is Hasan Sahih. Allah said: *and he calls Allah to witness as to that which is in his heart,* This Ayah indicates that such people pretend to be Muslims, but defy Allah by the disbelief and hypocrisy that their hearts conceal. This Tafsir was reported from Ibn `Abbas by Ibn Ishaq. It was also said that the Ayah means that when such people announce their Islam, they swear by Allah that what is in their hearts is the same of what their tongues are pronouncing. This is also a correct meaning for the Ayah that was chosen by `Abdur-Rahman bin Zayd bin Aslam. It is also the choice of Ibn Jarir who related it to Ibn `Abbas and Mujahid.

Allah said: *Yet he is the most Aladd of the opponents.* (2:204) The Ayah used the word Aladd here, which literally means `wicked' (here it means `quarrelsome'). Hence, a hypocrite lies, alters the truth when he quarrels and does not care for the truth. Rather, he deviates from the truth, deceives and becomes most quarrelsome. It is reported in Sahih that Allah's Messenger said: *The signs of a hypocrite are three: Whenever he speaks, he tells a lie. Whenever he promises, he always breaks it (his promise). If you have a dispute with him, he is most quarrelsome.*

Imam Bukhari reported that `A'ishah narrated that the Prophet said: *The most hated person to Allah is he who is Aladd and Khasim (meaning most quarrelsome).*

Allah then said: *And when he turns away, he struggles in the land to make mischief therein and to destroy the crops and the cattle, and Allah likes not mischief.*

This Ayah indicates that such persons are deviant in the tongue, evil in the deeds, their words are fabricated, their belief is wicked and their works are immoral. The Ayah used the (Arabic word) Sa`a (literally, `tries' or `intends'). This word was also used to describe Pharaoh. The hypocrite has no motive in this life but to cause mischief and to destroy the crops and the offspring, including what the animals produce and what the people depend on for their livelihood. Mujahid said, "If the hypocrite strives for mischief in the land, Allah prevents the rain from falling and thus the crops and the offspring perish." The Ayah continues: *and Allah likes not mischief.* that is, Allah does not like those who possess these characteristics, or those who act like this.

Allah said: *And when it is said to him, "Fear Allah'', he is led by arrogance to (more) crime.* This Ayah indicates that when the hypocrite, who deviates in his speech and deeds, is advised and commanded to fear Allah, refrain from his evil deeds and adhere to the truth, he refuses and becomes angry and outraged, as he is used to doing evil. This is why in this Ayah, Allah said: *So enough for him is Hell, and worst indeed is that place to rest* meaning, the Fire is enough punishment for the hypocrite.

3:7

It is He Who has sent down to you (Muhammad) the Book (this Qur'ân). In it are Verses that are entirely clear, they are the foundations of the Book [and those are the Verses of Al-Ahkâm (commandments), Al-Farâ'id (obligatory duties) and Al-Hudud (legal laws for the punishment of thieves, adulterers)]; and others not entirely clear. So as for those in whose hearts there is a deviation (from the truth) they follow that which is not entirely clear thereof, seeking Al-Fitnah (polytheism and trials), and seeking for its hidden meanings, but none knows its hidden meanings save Allâh. And those who are firmly grounded in knowledge say: "We believe in it; the whole of it (clear and unclear Verses) are from our Lord." And none receive admonition except men of understanding.

Allah states that in the Qur'an, there are Ayat that are Muhkamat, entirely clear and plain, and these are the foundations of the Book which are plain for everyone. And there are Ayat in the Qur'an that are Mutashabihat not entirely clear for many, or some people. So those who refer to the Muhkam Ayat to understand the Mutashabih Ayat, will have acquired the correct guidance, and vice versa. The Muhkamat are the Ayat that explain the abrogating rulings, the allowed, prohibited, laws, limits, obligations and rulings that should be believed in and implemented. As for the Mutashabihat Ayat, they include the abrogated Ayat, parables, oaths, and what should be believed in, but not implemented.

Muhammad bin Ishaq bin Yasar commented on, *In it are verses that are entirely clear* as "Containing proof of the Lord, immunity for the servants and a refutation of opponents and of falsehood. They cannot be changed or altered from what they were meant for." He also said, "As for the unclear Ayat, they can (but must not) be altered and changed, and this is a test from Allah to the servants, just as He tested them with the allowed and prohibited things. So these Ayat must not be altered to imply a false meaning or be distorted from the truth." Therefore, Allah said, *So as for those in whose hearts there is a deviation* meaning, those who are misguided and deviate from truth to falsehood, *they follow that which is not entirely clear thereof* meaning, they refer to the Mutashabih, because they are able to alter its meanings to conform with their false interpretation since the wordings of the Mutashabihat encompass such a wide area of meanings. As for the Muhkam Ayat, they cannot be altered because they are clear and, thus, constitute unequivocal proof against the misguided people.

Imam Ahmad recorded that `A'ishah said, "The Messenger of Allah recited, *It is He Who has sent down to you the Book. In it are verses that are entirely clear, they are the foundations of the Book; and others not entirely clear*, until, *Men of understanding* and he said, *When you see those who argue in it (using the Mutashabihat), then they are those whom Allah meant. Therefore, beware of them*." Al-Bukhari recorded a similar Hadith in the Tafsir of this Ayah 3:7, as did Muslim in the book of Qadar (the Divine Will) in his Sahih, and Abu Dawud in the Sunnah section of his Sunan, from `A'ishah; "The Messenger of Allah recited this Ayah, *It is He Who has sent down to you the Book. In it are verses that are entirely clear*, until, *And none receive admonition except men of understanding*. He then said, *When you see those who follow what is not so clear of the Qur'an, then they are those whom Allah described, so beware of them*." This is the wording recorded by Al-Bukhari.

Ibn `Abbas said: "Tafsir is of four types: Tafsir that the Arabs know in their language; Tafsir that no one is excused of being ignorant of; Tafsir that the scholars know; and Tafsir that only Allah knows."

3:156

O you who believe! Be not like those who disbelieve (hypocrites) and who say to their brethren when they travel through the earth or go out to fight: "If they had stayed with us, they would not have died or been killed," so that Allâh may make it a cause of regret in their hearts. It is Allâh that gives life and causes death. And Allâh is All¬Seer of what you do.

Allah forbids His believing servants from the disbelievers' false creed, seen in their statement about those who died in battle and during travel; "Had they abandoned these trips, they would not have met their demise."

3:167-168

And that He might test the hypocrites, it was said to them: "Come, fight in the Way of Allâh or (at least) defend yourselves." They said: "Had we known that fighting will take place, we would certainly have followed you." They were that day, nearer to disbelief than to Faith, saying with their mouths what was not in their hearts. And Allâh has full knowledge of what they conceal. (167) (They are) the ones who said about their killed brethren while they themselves sat (at home): "If only they had listened to us, they would not have been killed." Say: "Avert death from your ownselves, if you speak the truth."

This refers to the Companions of `Abdullah bin Ubayy bin Salul who went back (to Al-Madinah) with him before the battle. Some believers followed them and encouraged them to come back and fight, saying, *or defend*, so that the number of Muslims increases, as Ibn `Abbas, `Ikrimah, Sa`id bin Jubayr, Ad-Dahhak, Abu Salih, Al-Hasan and As-Suddi stated. Al-Hasan bin Salih said that this part of the Ayah means, help by supplicating for us, while others said it means, man the posts. However, they refused, saying, "*Had we known that fighting will take place, we would certainly have followed you.*" meaning, according to Mujahid, if we knew that you would fight today, we would join you, but we think you will not fight.

24

Allah said, *They were that day, nearer to disbelief than to faith,* This Ayah indicates that a person passes through various stages, sometimes being closer to Kufr and sometimes closer to faith. Allah then said, *saying with their mouths what was not in their hearts.* for they utter what they do not truly believe in. They knew that there was an army of idolators that came from a far land raging against the Muslims, to avenge their noble men whom the Muslims killed in Badr. These idolators came in larger numbers than the Muslims, so it was clear that a battle will certainly occur. Mujahid said that Jabir bin `Abdullah said, "This Ayah 3:168 was revealed about `Abdullah bin Ubayy bin Salul (the chief hypocrite)."

3:173

Those (i.e. believers) unto whom the people (hypocrites) said, "Verily, the people (pagans) have gathered against you (a great army), therefore, fear them." But it (only) increased them in Faith, and they said: "Allâh (Alone) is Sufficient for us, and He is the Best Disposer of affairs (for us)."

Al-Bukhari recorded that Ibn `Abbas said,

"Allah Alone is Sufficient for us and He is the Best Disposer of affairs for us.'"

"Ibrahim said it when he was thrown in fire. Muhammad said it when the people said, `*Verily, the people have gathered against you, therefore, fear them.*' *But it only increased them in faith, and they said, `Allah is Sufficient for us and He is the Best Disposer of affairs for us.*'" Abu Bakr Ibn Marduwyah recorded that Anas bin Malik said that the Prophet was told on the day of Uhud, "*Verily, the people have gathered against you, therefore, fear them.*" Thereafter, Allah sent down this Ayah

Hypocrites have always threatened the Muslims, saying that the disbelievers have amassed against them, in order to instill fear in them, but this does not worry true believers, rather, they trust in Allah and seek His help.

4:60-66

Have you seen those (hyprocrites) who claim that they believe in that which has been sent down to you, and that which was sent down before you, and they wish to go for judgement (in their disputes) to the Tâghût (false judges) while they have been ordered to reject them. But Shaitân (Satan) wishes to lead them far astray. (60)And when it is said to them: "Come to what Allâh has sent down and to the Messenger (Muhammud)," you see the hypocrites turn away from you with aversion (61) How then, when a catastrophe befalls them because of what their hands have sent forth, they come to you swearing by Allâh, "We meant no more than goodwill and conciliation!" (62) They (hypocrites) are those of whom Allâh knows what is in their hearts; so turn aside from them (do not punish them) but admonish them, and speak to them an effective word (i.e. to believe in Allâh, worship Him, obey Him, and be afraid of Him) to reach their innerselves (63) We sent no Messenger, but to be obeyed by Allâh's Leave. If they (hypocrites), when they had been unjust to themselves, had come to you (Muhammad) and begged Allâh's Forgiveness, and the Messenger had begged forgiveness for them: indeed, they would have found Allâh All-Forgiving (One Who forgives and accepts repentance),

Most Merciful. (64) But no, by your Lord, they can have no Faith, until they make you (O Muhammad) judge in all disputes between them, and find in themselves no resistance against your decisions, and accept (them) with full submission. (65) And if We had ordered them (saying), "Kill yourselves (i.e. the innnocent ones kill the guilty ones) or leave your homes," very few of them would have done it; but if they had done what they were told, it would have been better for them, and would have strengthened their (Faith);

Allah chastises those who claim to believe in what Allah has sent down to His Messenger and to the earlier Prophets, yet they refer to other than the Book of Allah and the Sunnah of His Messenger for judgment in various disputes. It was reported that the reason behind revealing this Ayah was that a man from the Ansar and a Jew had a dispute, and the Jew said, "Let us refer to Muhammad to judge between us." However, the Muslim man said, "Let us refer to Ka`b bin Al-Ashraf (a Jew) to judge between us." It was also reported that the Ayah was revealed about some hypocrites who pretended to be Muslims, yet they sought to refer to the judgment of Jahiliyyah. Other reasons were also reported behind the revelation of the Ayah. However, the Ayah has a general meaning, as it chastises all those who refrain from referring to the Qur'an and Sunnah for judgment and prefer the judgment of whatever they chose of falsehood, which befits the description of Taghut here.

At-Tabarani recorded that Ibn `Abbas said, "Abu Barzah Al-Aslami used to be a soothsayer who judged between the Jews in their disputes. When some Muslims came to him to judge between them, Allah sent down, *Have you not seen those (hyprocrites) who claim that they believe in that which has been sent down to you, and that which was sent down before you*), until, *"We meant no more than goodwill and conciliation!"* apologizing and swearing that they only sought goodwill and reconciliation when they referred to other than the Prophet for judgment, not that they believe in such alternative judgment, as they claim. Allah then said, *They (hypocrites) are those of whom Allah knows what is in their hearts;* These people are hypocrites, and Allah knows what is in their hearts and will punish them accordingly, for nothing escapes Allah's watch.

Allah's statement, *If they (hypocrites), when they had been unjust to themselves,* directs the sinners and evildoers, when they commit errors and mistakes, to come to the Messenger , so that they ask Allah for forgiveness in his presence and ask him to supplicate to Allah to forgive them. If they do this, Allah will forgive them and award them His mercy and pardon. Allah said, *But no, by your Lord, they can have no faith, until they make you judge in all disputes between them*, Allah swears by His Glorious, Most Honorable Self, that no one shall attain faith until he refers to the Messenger for judgment in all matters. Thereafter, whatever the Messenger commands, is the plain truth that must be submitted to inwardly and outwardly.

Al-Bukhari recorded that `Urwah said, "Az-Zubayr quarreled with a man about a stream which both of them used for irrigation. Allah's Messenger said to Az-Zubayr,

(O Zubayr! Irrigate (your garden) first, and then let the water flow to your neighbor.) The Ansari became angry and said, `O Allah's Messenger! Is it because he is your cousin' On that, the face of Allah's Messenger changed color (because of anger) and said,

(Irrigate (your garden), O Zubayr, and then withhold the water until it reaches the walls (surrounding the palms). Then, release the water to your neighbor.) So, Allah's Messenger gave Az-Zubayr his full right when the Ansari made him angry. Before that, Allah's Messenger had given a generous judgment, beneficial for Az-Zubayr and the Ansari. Az-Zubayr said, `I think the following verse was revealed concerning that case, *But no, by your Lord, they can have no faith, until they make you (O Muhammad) judge in all disputes between them.* '''

Another reason in his Tafsir, Al-Hafiz Abu Ishaq Ibrahim bin `Abdur-Rahman bin Ibrahim bin Duhaym recorded that Damrah narrated that two men took their dispute to the Prophet , and he gave a judgment to the benefit of whoever among them had the right. The person who lost the dispute said, "I do not agree." The other person asked him, "What do you want then" He said, "Let us go to Abu Bakr As-Siddiq." They went to Abu Bakr and the person who won the dispute said, "We went to the Prophet with our dispute and he issued a decision in my favor." Abu Bakr said, "Then the decision is that which the Messenger of Allah issued." The person who lost the dispute still rejected the decision and said, "Let us go to `Umar bin Al-Khattab." When they went to `Umar, the person who won the dispute said, "We took our dispute to the Prophet and he decided in my favor, but this man refused to submit to the decision." `Umar bin Al-Khattab asked the second man and he concurred. `Umar went to his house and emerged from it holding aloft his sword. He struck the head of the man who rejected the Prophet's decision with the sword and killed him.

Allah states that even if the people were commanded to commit what they were prohibited from doing, most of them would not submit to this command, for their wicked nature is such that they dispute orders. Allah has complete knowledge of what has not occurred, and how it would be if and when it did occur. This is why Allah said,

And if We had ordered them (saying), "Kill yourselves (i.e. the innocent ones kill the guilty ones until the end of the Ayah.

4:72

There is certainly among you he who would linger behind (from Jihad). If a misfortune befalls you, he says, "Indeed Allâh has favored me in that I was not present among them."

Mujahid and others said that this Ayah was revealed about the hypocrites. Muqatil bin Hayyan said that, *linger behind* means, stays behind and does not join Jihad. It is also possible that this person himself lingers behind, while luring others away from joining Jihad. For instance, `Abdullah bin Ubayy bin Salul, may Allah curse him, used to linger behind and lure other people to do the same and refrain from joining Jihad, as Ibn Jurayj and Ibn Jarir stated.

4:77-78

Have you not seen those who were told to hold back their hands (from fighting) and perform As-Salât (Iqâmat-as-Salât), and give Zakât but when the fighting was ordained for them, behold! a section of them fear men as they fear Allâh or even more. They say: "Our Lord! Why have you ordained for us fighting? Would that You had granted us respite for a short period?" Say: "Short is the enjoyment of this world. The Hereafter is (far) better for him who fears Allâh, and you shall not be dealt with unjustly even equal to a scalish thread in the long slit of a date-stone. (77) "Wheresoever you may be, death will overtake you even if you are in fortresses built up strong and high!" And if some good reaches them, they say, "This is from Allâh," but if some evil befalls them, they say, "This is from you (O Muhammad)." Say: "All things are from Allâh," so what is wrong with these people that they fail to understand any word?

When the command to fight was revealed, just as Muslims wished, some of them became weary and were very fearful of facing the idolators in battle.

They say: "Our Lord! Why have You ordained for us fighting Would that You had granted us respite for a short period'' meaning, we wish that Jihad was delayed until a later time, because it means bloodshed, orphans and widows.

Allah said, *And if some good reaches them* meaning, fertile years and provision of fruits, produce, children, etc., as said by Ibn `Abbas, Abu Al-`Aliyah and As-Suddi.

they say, "This is from Allah," but *if some evil befalls them* drought, famine, shortages of fruits and produce, death that strikes their children or animals, and so forth, as Abu Al-`Aliyah and As-Suddi stated. *they say, "This is from you,"* meaning, because of you and because we followed you and embraced your religion.

4:88-91

Then what is the matter with you that you are divided into two parties about the hypocrites? Allâh has cast them back (to disbelief) because of what they have earned. Do you want to guide him whom Allâh has made to go astray? And he whom Allâh has made to go astray, you will never find for him any way (of guidance). (88) They wish that you reject Faith, as they have rejected (Faith), and thus that you all become equal (like one another). So take not Auliyâ' (protectors or friends) from them, till they emigrate in the Way of Allâh. But if they turn back (from Islâm), take (hold of) them and kill them wherever you find them, and take neither Auliyâ' (protectors or friends) nor helpers from them. (89) Except those who join a group, between you and whom there is a treaty (of peace), or those who approach you with their breasts restraining from fighting you as well as fighting their own people. Had Allâh willed, indeed He would have given them power over you, and they would have fought you. So if they withdraw from you, and fight not against you, and offer you peace, then Allâh has opened no way for you against them. (90) You will find others that wish to have

32

security from you and security from their people. Every time they are sent back to temptation, they yield thereto. If they withdraw not from you, nor offer you peace, nor restrain their hands, take (hold of) them and kill them wherever you find them. In their case, We have provided you with a clear warrant against them.

Allah criticizes the believers for disagreeing over the hypocrites. There are conflicting opinions over the reason behind revealing this Ayah. Imam Ahmad recorded that Zayd bin Thabit said the Messenger of Allah marched towards Uhud. However, some people who accompanied him went back to Al-Madinah, and the Companions of the Messenger of Allah divided into two groups concerning them, one saying they should be killed and the other objecting. Allah sent down, *Then what is the matter with you that you are divided into two parties about the hypocrites*

The Messenger of Allah said, *She (Al-Madinah) is Taybah, and she expels filth, just as the billow expels rust from iron.* The Two Sahihs also recorded this Hadith. Al-`Awfi reported that Ibn `Abbas said that the Ayah was revealed about some people in Makkah who said they embraced Islam, yet they gave their support to the idolators. One time, these people went out of Makkah to fulfill some needs and said to each other, "If we meet the Companions of Muhammad, there will be no harm for us from their side." When the believers got news that these people went out of Makkah, some of them said, "Let us march to these cowards and kill them, because they support your enemy against you." However, another group from the believers said, "Glory be to Allah! Do you kill a people who say as you have said, just because they did not perform Hijrah or leave their land? Is it allowed to shed their blood and confiscate their money in this case?" So they divided to two groups, while the Messenger was with them, and did not prohibit either group from reiterating their argument.

Thereafter, Allah revealed, *Then what is the matter with you that you are divided into two parties about the hypocrites*) Ibn Abi Hatim recorded this Hadith. Allah said, *Allah has cast them back because of what they have earned.* meaning, He made them revert to, and fall into error. Ibn `Abbas said that, *Arkasahum* means, `cast them'. Allah's statement, *because of what they have earned* means, because of their defiance and disobedience to the Messenger and following falsehood.

Allah's statement, *They wish that you reject faith, as they have rejected, and thus that you all become equal.* means, they wish that you fall into misguidance, so that you and they are equal in that regard. This is because of their enmity and hatred for you. Thus Allah said, *So take not Awliya' from them, till they emigrate in the way of Allah. But if they turn back*, if they abandon Hijrah, as Al-`Awfi reported from Ibn `Abbas.

Allah excluded some people; *Except those who join a group, between you and whom there is a treaty (of peace)* meaning, except those who join and take refuge with a people with whom you have a pact of peace, or people of Dhimmah, then treat them as you treat the people with whom you have peace. This is the saying of As-Suddi, Ibn Zayd and Ibn Jarir.

In his Sahih, Al-Bukhari recorded the story of the treaty of Al-Hudaybiyyah, where it was mentioned that whoever liked to have peace with Quraysh and conduct a pact with them, then they were allowed. Those who liked to have peace with Muhammad and his Companions and enter a pact with them were allowed. It was reported that Ibn `Abbas said that this Ayah was later abrogated.

Allah's statement: *You will find others that wish to have security from you and security from their people.* refers to a type of people who on the surface appear to be like the type we just mentioned. However, the intention of each type is different, for the latter are hypocrites. They pretend to be Muslims with the Prophet and his Companions, so that they could attain safety with the Muslims for their blood, property and families. However, they support the idolators in secret and worship what they worship, so that they are at peace with them also. These people have secretly sided with the idolators.

Allah said, *Every time they are sent back to Fitnah, they yield thereto.* meaning, they dwell in Fitnah. As-Suddi said that the Fitnah mentioned here refers to Shirk. Ibn Jarir recorded that Mujahid said that the Ayah was revealed about a group from Makkah who used to go to the Prophet in Al-Madinah pretending to be Muslims. However, when they went back to Quraysh, they reverted to worshipping idols. They wanted to be at peace with both sides. Allah commanded they should be fought against, unless they withdraw from combat and resort to peace.

Verily! As for those whom the angels take (in death) while they are wronging themselves (as they stayed among the disbelievers even though emigration was obligatory for them), they (angels) say (to them): "In what (condition) were you?" They reply: "We were weak and oppressed on earth." They (angels) say: "Was not the earth of Allâh spacious enough for you to emigrate therein?" Such men will find their abode in Hell - What an evil destination!

Al-Bukhari recorded that Muhammad bin `Abdur-Rahman, Abu Al-Aswad, said, "The people of Al-Madinah were forced to prepare an army (to fight against the people of Ash-Sham during the Khilafah of Abdullah bin Az-Zubayir at Makkah), and I was enlisted in it. Then I met `Ikrimah, the freed slave of Ibn `Abbas, and informed him (about it), and he forbade me strongly from doing so (i.e., to enlist in that army), and then he said to me, `Ibn `Abbas told me that some Muslims used to go out with the idolators increasing the size of their army against the Messenger of Allah . Then, an arrow would hit one of them and kill him, or he would be struck on his neck (with a sword) and killed, and Allah sent down the Ayah, *Verily, as for those whom the angels take (in death) while they are wronging themselves.*" Ad-Dahhak stated that this Ayah was revealed about some hypocrites who did not join the Messenger of Allah but remained in Makkah and went out with the idolators for the battle of Badr. They were killed among those who were killed. Thus, this honorable Ayah was revealed about those who reside among the idolators, while able to perform Hijrah. Such people will be committing injustice against themselves and falling into a prohibition according to the consensus and also according to this Ayah.

4:137-146

Verily, those who believe, then disbelieve, then believe (again), and (again) disbelieve, and go on increasing in disbelief; Allâh will not forgive them, nor guide them on the (Right) Way (137) Give to the hypocrites the tidings that there is for them a painful torment. (138) Those who take disbelievers for Auliyâ' (protectors or helpers or friends) instead of believers, do they seek honour, power and glory with them? Verily, then to Allâh belongs all honour, power and glory. (139) And it has already been revealed to you in the Book (this Qur'ân) that when you hear the Verses of Allâh being denied and mocked at, then sit not with them, until they engage in a talk other than that; (but if you stayed with them) certainly in that case you would be like them. Surely, Allâh will collect the hypocrites and disbelievers all together in Hell, (140) Those (hyprocrites) who wait and watch about you; if you gain a victory from Allâh, they say: "Were we not with you?" But if the disbelievers gain a success, they say (to them): "Did we not gain mastery over you and did we not protect you from the believers?" Allâh will judge between you (all) on the Day of Resurrection. And never will Allâh grant to the disbelievers a way (to triumph) over the believers. (141) Verily, the hypocrites seek to deceive Allâh, but it is He Who deceives them. And when they stand up for As-Salât (the prayer), they stand with laziness and to be seen of men, and they do not remember Allâh but little. (142) (They are) swaying between this and that, belonging neither to these nor to those, and he whom Allâh sends astray, you will not find for him a way (to the truth - Islâm). (143) O you who believe! Take not for Auliyâ' (protectors or helpers or friends) disbelievers instead of believers. Do you wish to offer Allâh a manifest proof against yourselves? (144) Verily, the hyprocrites will be in the lowest depths (grade) of the Fire; no helper will you find for them. (145) Except those who repent (from hypocrisy), do righteous good deeds, hold fast to Allâh, and purify their religion for Allâh (by worshipping none but Allâh, and do good for Allâh's sake only, not to show off), then they will be with the believers. And Allâh will grant the believers a great reward.

Allah states that whoever embraces the faith, reverts from it, embraces it again, reverts from it and remains on disbelief and increases in it until death, then he will never have a chance to gain accepted repentance after death. Nor will Allah forgive him, or deliver him from his plight to the path of correct guidance. Ibn Abi Hatim recorded that his father said that Ahmad bin `Abdah related that Hafs bin Jami' said that Samak said that `Ikrimah reported that Ibn `Abbas commented; *and go on increasing in disbelief,* "They remain on disbelief until they die." Mujahid said similarly.

Allah then said, *Give to the hypocrites the tidings that there is for them a painful torment.* Hence, the hypocrites have this characteristic, for they believe, then disbelieve, and this is why their hearts become sealed. Allah describes the hypocrites as taking the disbelievers as friends instead of the believers, meaning they are the disbelievers' supporters in reality, for they give them their loyalty and friendship in secret. They also say to disbelievers when they are alone with them, "We are with you, we only mock the believers by pretending to follow their religion."

Allah's statement, *And it has already been revealed to you in the Book that when you hear the verses of Allah being denied and mocked at, then sit not with them, until they engage in talk other than that; certainly in that case you would be like them.* The Ayah means, if you still commit this prohibition after being aware of its prohibition, sitting with them where Allah's Ayat are rejected, mocked at and denied, and you sanction such conduct, then you have participated with them in what they are doing. So Allah said,(*But if you stayed with them) certainly in that case you would be like them.*) concerning the burden they will earn.

Allah's statement, *Surely, Allah will collect the hypocrites and disbelievers all together in Hell.* means, just as the hypocrites participate in the Kufr of disbelievers, Allah will join them all together to reside in the Fire for eternity, dwelling in torment, punishment, enchained, restrained and in drinking boiling water.

Allah states that the hypocrites watch and await the harm that occurs to the believers, awaiting the time when the Muslim circumstances and religion are dissolved and the state of Kufr takes over.

Allah will judge between you (all) on the Day of Resurrection meaning, by what He knows about you, O hypocrites. Therefore, do not be deceived by being shaded under the protection of Islamic Law in this life, which is such only out of Allah's wisdom. Surely, on the Day of Resurrection, your pretending shall not benefit you, because on that Day, the secrets of the souls will be disclosed and the contents of the hearts will be collected. Allah said,

And never will Allah grant to the disbelievers a way (to triumph) over the believers. `Abdur-Razzaq recorded that Yasi` Al-Kindi said, "A man came to `Ali bin Abi Talib and said, `What about this Ayah, *And never will Allah grant to the disbelievers a way (to triumph) over the believers.* `Ali said, `Come closer, come closer. Allah will judge between you on the Day of Resurrection, and He will not grant victory for the disbelievers over the believers.' " Ibn Jurayj recorded that `Ata' Al-Khurasani said that Ibn `Abbas said that, *And never will Allah grant to the disbelievers a way (to triumph) over the believers.* "Will occur on the Day of Resurrection." As-Suddi recorded that Abu Malik Al-Ashja`i said that it occurs on the Day of Resurrection. As-Suddi said that "way" means, proof. It is possible that the meaning of, `and never will Allah grant to the disbelievers a way (to triumph) over the believers', is in this life by being unable to exterminate the believers completely, although they sometimes gain victory over some Muslims. However, the Final Triumph will be for the believers in this life and the Hereafter.

Verily, the hypocrites seek to deceive Allah, but it is He Who deceives them. There is no doubt that Allah can never be deceived, for He has perfect knowledge of the secrets and what the hearts conceal. However, the hypocrites, due to their ignorance, scarce knowledge and weak minds, think that since they were successful in deceiving people, using Islamic Law as a cover of safety for themselves, they will acquire the same status with Allah on the Day of Resurrection and deceive Him too. Allah states that on that Day, the hypocrites will swear to Him that they were on the path of righteousness and correctness thinking that such statement will benefit them with Allah.

Allah's statement, *And when they stand up for Salah, they stand with laziness*. This is the characteristic of the hypocrites with the most honored, best and righteous act of worship, the prayer. When they stand for prayer, they stand in laziness because they neither truly intend to perform it nor do they believe in it, have humility in it, or understand it. This is the description of their outward attitude! As for their hearts, Allah said, *to be seen of men* meaning, they do not have sincerity when worshipping Allah. Rather, they show off to people so that they gain closeness to them. They are often absent from the prayers that they can hide away from, such as the `Isha' prayer and the Dawn prayer that are prayed in darkness. In the Two Sahihs, it is recorded that the Messenger of Allah said, *The heaviest prayers on the hypocrites are the `Isha' and Dawn prayers. If they know their rewards, they will attend them even if they have to crawl. I was about to order someone to pronounce the Adhan for the prayer, then order someone to lead the prayer for the people, then order some men to collect fire-wood (fuel); then I would burn the houses around men who did not attend the (compulsory congregational) prayer.)* In another narration, the Prophet said, *By Him, in Whose Hand my soul is, if anyone of them had known that he would get a bone*

41

covered with good meat or two (small) pieces of meat between two ribs, he would have turned up for the prayer, and had it not been that the houses have women and children in them, I would burn their homes around them.

Allah's statement, *And they do not remember Allah but little* means, during the prayer they do not feel humbleness or pay attention to what they are reciting. Rather, during their prayer, they are inattentive, jesting and avoid the good that they are meant to receive from prayer. Imam Malik reported that Al-`Ala' bin `Abdur-Rahman said that Anas bin Malik said that the Messenger of Allah said, *This is the prayer of the hypocrite, this is the prayer of the hypocrite, this is the prayer of the hypocrite. He sits watching the sun until when it goes down between the two horns of the devil, he stands up pecks out four Rak`ahs (for `Asr) without remembering Allah during them except little.*) Muslim, At-Tirmidhi and An-Nasa'i also recorded it. At-Tirmidhi said "Hasan Sahih".

Allah then forbids His believing servants from taking the disbelievers as friends instead of the believers. This includes being friends and associates of the disbelievers, advising them, being intimate with them and exposing the secrets of the believers to them.

Ibn Jarir recorded that `Abdullah bin Mas`ud said that, *Verily, the hypocrites will be in the lowest depths (grade) of the Fire,* "Inside coffins of Fire that surround them, for they are closed and sealed in them." Ibn Abi Hatim recorded that when Ibn Mas`ud was asked about the hypocrites, he said,

"They will be placed in coffins made of fire and they will be closed in them in the lowest depth of the Fire."

5:51-53

O you who believe! Take not the Jews and the Christians as Auliyâ' (friends, protectors, helpers), they are but Auliyâ' of each other. And if any amongst you takes them (as Auliyâ'), then surely he is one of them. Verily, Allâh guides not those people who are the Zâlimûn (polytheists and wrong-doers and unjust). (51) And you see those in whose hearts there is a disease (of hypocrisy), they hurry to their friendship, saying: "We fear lest some misfortune of a disaster may befall us." Perhaps Allâh may bring a victory or a decision according to His Will. Then they will become regretful for what they have been keeping as a secret in themselves. (52) And those who believe will say: "Are these the men (hypocrites) who swore their strongest oaths by Allâh that they were with you (Muslims)?" All that they did has been in vain (because of their hypocrisy), and they have become the losers.

Allah forbids His believing servants from having Jews and Christians as friends, because they are the enemies of Islam and its people, may Allah curse them. Allah then states that they are friends of each other and He gives a warning threat to those who do this, *And if any among you befriends them, then surely he is one of them.* Ibn Abi Hatim recorded that `Umar ordered Abu Musa Al-Ash`ari to send him one sheet of balance the count of what he took in and what he spent. Abu Musa then had a Christian scribe, and he was able to comply with `Umar's demand. `Umar liked what he saw and exclaimed, "This scribe is proficient. Would you read in the

Masjid a letter that came to us from Ash-Sham" Abu Musa said, `He cannot." `Umar said, "Is he not pure" Abu Musa said, "No, but he is Christian." Abu Musa said, "So `Umar admonished me and poked my thigh (with his finger), saying, `Drive him out (from Al-Madinah).' He then recited, *O you who believe! Take not the Jews and the Christians as friends...*" Then he reported that `Abdullah bin `Utbah said, "Let one of you beware that he might be a Jew or a Christian, while unaware."

And you see those in whose hearts there is a disease... A disease of doubt, hesitation and hypocrisy. *they hurry to their friendship,* meaning, they rush to offer them their friendship and allegiances in secret and in public, saying: "We fear lest some misfortune of a disaster may befall us." They thus offer this excuse for their friendship and allegiances to the disbelievers, saying that they fear that the disbelievers might defeat the Muslims, so they want to be in favor with the Jews and Christians, to use this favor for their benefit in that eventuality! *Then they will become* meaning, the hypocrites who gave their friendship to the Jews and Christians, will become, *for what they have been keeping as a secret in themselves* of allegiances, *regretful,* for their friendship with the Jews and Christians which did not benefit them or protect them from any harm. Rather, it was nothing but harm, as Allah exposed their true reality to His faithful servants in this life, although they tried to conceal it. When the signs that exposed their hypocrisy were compiled against them, their matter became clear to Allah's faithful servants. So the believers were amazed at these hypocrites who pretended to be believers, swearing to their faithfulness, yet their claims were all lies and deceit.

8:49

When the hypocrites and those in whose hearts was a disease said: "These people (Muslims) are deceived by their religion." But whoever puts his trust in Allâh, then surely, Allâh is All-Mighty, All-Wise

Ali bin Abi Talhah said that Ibn `Abbas commented, "When the two armies (at Badr) drew closer to each other, Allah made the Muslims look few in the eyes of the idolators and the idolators look few in the eyes of the Muslims. The idolators said,

These people (Muslims) are deceived by their religion. because they thought that Muslims were so few. They believed, without doubt, that they would defeat the Muslims. Allah said, *But whoever puts his trust in Allah, then surely, Allah is All-Mighty, All-Wise.* Qatadah commented, "They saw a group of believers who came in defense of Allah's religion. We were informed that when he saw Muhammad and his Companions, Abu Jahl said, `By Allah! After this day, they will never worship Allah!' He said this in viciousness and transgression." `Amir Ash-Sha`bi said, "Some people from Makkah were considering embracing Islam, but when they went with the idolators to Badr and saw how few the Muslims were, they said, *These people (Muslims) are deceived by their religion.*

9:42

Had it been a near gain (booty in front of them) and an easy journey, they would have followed you, but the distance was long for them, and they would swear by Allâh, "If we only could, we would certainly have come forth with you." They destroy their ownselves, and Allâh knows that they are liars –

Allah admonishes those who lagged behind and did not join the Prophet for the battle of Tabuk, those who asked the Prophet for permission to remain behind, falsely pretending to have legitimate reasons.

9:45-50

It is only those who believe not in Allâh and the Last Day and whose hearts are in doubt that ask your leave (to be exempted from Jihâd). So in their doubts they waver. (45) And if they had intended to march out, certainly, they would have made some preparation for it, but Allâh was averse to their being sent forth, so He made them lag behind, and it was said (to them), "Sit you among those who sit (at home)." (46) Had they marched out with you, they would have added to you nothing except disorder, and they would have hurried about in your midst (spreading corruption) and sowing sedition among you, and there are some among you who would have listened to them. And Allâh is the All-Knower of the Zâlimûn (polytheists and wrong-doers). (47) Verily, they had plotted sedition before, and had upset matters for you, - until the truth (victory) came and the Decree of Allâh (His religion, Islâm) became manifest though they hated it (48) And among them is he who says: "Grant me leave (to be exempted from

Jihâd) and put me not into trial." Surely, they have fallen into trial. And verily, Hell is surrounding the disbelievers. If good befalls you, it grieves them, but if a calamity overtakes you, they say: "We took our precaution beforehand," and they turn away rejoicing.

Muhammad bin Ishaq said, "Those who sought permission (from the Messenger to lag behind) included some of the chiefs, such as `Abdullah bin Ubayy bin Salul and Al-Jadd bin Qays, who were masters of their people. Allah also made them lag behind because He knew that if they went along with the Messenger they would sow sedition in his army." There were some in the Prophet's army who liked these chiefs and were ready to obey them, because they considered them honorable. Muhammad bin Ishaq also reported from Az-Zuhri, Yazid bin Ruwman, `Abdullah bin Abi Bakr, `Asim bin Qatadah and several others that they said, "The Messenger of Allah said to Al-Jadd bin Qays from Bani Salimah, `Would you like to fight the yellow ones (Romans) this year) He said, `O Allah's Messenger! Give me permission (to remain behind and do not cause Fitnah for me. By Allah! My people know that there is not a man who is more fond of women than I. I fear that if I see the women of the yellow ones, I would not be patient.' The Messenger of Allah turned away from him and said, I give you permission. In Al-Jadd's case, this Ayah was revealed, And among them is he who says: "Grant me leave and put me not into trial.''* Therefore, Allah says that the Fitnah that he fell into because of not joining the Messenger of Allah (in Jihad) and preferring his safety to the safety of the Messenger is worse than the Fitnah that he falsely claimed to fear." It was reported from Ibn `Abbas, Mujahid and several others that this Ayah was revealed in the case of Al-Jadd bin Qays, who was among the chiefs of Bani Salimah. It is also recorded in the Sahih that the Messenger of Allah asked, *Who is your chief, O Bani Salamah They said, "Al-Jadd bin Qays, although we consider him a miser." The Messenger of Allah said, There is not a disease worse than stinginess! Therefore, your chief is the white young man with curly hair, Bishr bin Al-Bara' bin Ma'rur.*

If a blessing, such as victory and triumph over the enemies, is given to the Prophet , thus pleasing him and his Companions, it grieves the hypocrites.

9:53-58

Say: "Spend (in Allâh's Cause) willingly or unwillingly, it will not be accepted from you. Verily, you are ever a people who are Fâsiqûn (rebellious, disobedient to Allâh)." (53) And nothing prevents their contributions from being accepted from them except that they disbelieved in Allâh and in His Messenger (Muhammad); and that they came not to As-Salât (the prayer) except in a lazy state; and that they offer not contributions but unwillingly. (54) So let not their wealth or their children amaze you (O Muhammad); in reality Allâh's Plan is to punish them with these things in the life of the this world, and that their souls shall depart (die) while they are disbelievers. (55) They swear by Allâh that they are truly of you while they are not of you, but they are a people (hypocrites) who are afraid (that you may kill them). (56) Should they find a refuge, or caves, or a place of concealment, they would turn straightway thereto with a swift rush. (57) And of them are some who accuse you (O Muhammad) in the matter of

48

(the distribution of) the alms. If they are given part thereof, they are pleased, but if they are not given thereof, behold! They are enraged!

Allah mentions the reason behind not accepting their charity from them, *except that they disbelieved in Allah and in His Messenger.* and the deeds are accepted if they are preceded with faith, *and that they came not to the Salah except in a lazy state.* Therefore, they neither have good intention nor eagerness to perform the acts of faith, *And nothing prevents their contributions from being accepted from them except that they disbelieved in Allah and in His Messenger, and that they came not to the Salah (the prayer) except in a lazy state, and that they offer not contributions but unwillingly.* The Truthful, to whom the Truth was revealed, Muhammad, peace be upon him, said that Allah does not stop giving rewards until you (believers) stop performing good deeds, and that Allah is Tayyib Good and Pure and only accepts what is Tayyib. This is why Allah does not accept charity or good deeds from the people described in these Ayat, because He only accepts it from those who have Taqwa.

Hypocrites prefer not to mix with Muslims, but necessity has its rules. It is because of this that they feel grief, sadness and sorrow, seeing Islam and its people enjoying ever more might, triumph and glory. Therefore, whatever pleases Muslims brings them grief, and this is why they prefer to disassociate themselves from the believers.

Qatadah commented on Allah's statement, *And of them are some who accuse you concerning the alms.* "Allah says, `Some of them question your integrity in the matter of distribution of the alms.' We were told that a bedouin man, who had recently embraced Islam, came to the Prophet , when he was dividing some gold and silver, and said to him, `O Muhammad! Even though Allah commanded you to divide in fairness, you have not done so.' The Prophet of Allah said, *Woe to you! Who would be fair to you after me then?* The Prophet of Allah said next, *Beware of this man and his likes! There are similar persons in my Ummah who recite the Qur'an, but the Qur'an will not go beyond their throat. If they rise (against Muslims rulers) then kill them, if they rise, kill them, then if they rise kill them.* We were also told that the Prophet of Allah used to say, *By He in Whose Hand is my life! I do not give or withhold anything; I am only a keeper.*" This statement from Qatadah is similar to the Hadith that the Two Shaykhs narrated from Abu Sa`id about the story of Dhul-Khuwaysirah, whose name was Hurqus. Hurqus protested against the Prophet's division of the war spoils of Hunayn, saying, "Be fair, for you have not been fair!" The Prophet said, *I would have become a loser and a failure if I was not fair!* The Messenger said after that man left, *Among the offspring of this man will be some with whose prayer, when one of you sees it, would belittle his prayer, and his fast as compared to their fast. They will be renegades from the religion, just like an arrow goes through the game's body. Wherever you find them, kill them, for verily, they are the worst dead people under the cover of the sky.*

9:61-68

And among them are men who annoy the Prophet (Muhammad) and say: "He is (lending his) ear (to every news)." Say: "He listens to what is best for you; he believes in Allâh; has faith in the believers; and is a mercy to those of you who believe." But those who hurt Allâh's Messenger (Muhammad) will have a painful torment. (61) They swear by Allâh to you (Muslims) in order to please you, but it is more fitting that they should please Allâh and His Messenger (Muhammad), if they are believers. (62) Know they not that whoever opposes and shows hostility to Allâh and His Messenger, certainly for him will be the Fire of Hell to abide therein. That is extreme disgrace. (63) The hypocrites fear lest a Sûrah (chapter of the Qur'ân) should be revealed about them, showing them what is in their hearts. Say: "(Go ahead and) mock! But certainly Allâh will bring to light all that you fear." (64) If you ask them (about this), they declare: "We were only talking idly and joking." Say: "Was it at Allâh (swt), and His Ayât (proofs, evidences, verses, lessons, signs, revelations) and His Messenger that you were mocking?" (65) Make no excuse; you have disbelieved after you had believed. If We pardon some of you, We will punish others amongst you because they were Mujrimûn (disbelievers, polytheists, sinners, criminals). (66) The hypocrites, men and women, are one from another, they enjoin (on the people) Al-Munkar (i.e. disbelief and polytheism of all kinds and all that Islâm has forbidden), and forbid (people) from Al-Ma'rûf (i.e. Islâmic Monotheism and all that Islâm orders one to do), and they close their hands [from giving (spending in Allâh's Cause) alms]. They have forgotten Allâh, so He has forgotten them. Verily, the hypocrites are the Fâsiqûn (rebellious, disobedient to Allâh). (67) Allâh has promised the hypocrites — men and women — and the *disbelievers, the Fire of Hell, therein shall they abide. It will suffice them. Allâh has cursed them and for them is the lasting torment.*

Allah says, some hypocrites bother the Messenger of Allah by questioning his character, saying, *he is (lending his) ear*, to those who say anything about us; he believes whoever talks to him. Therefore, if we went to him and swore, he would believe us. Similar was reported from Ibn `Abbas, Mujahid and Qatadah.

Qatadah said about Allah's statement, *They swear by Allah to you (Muslims) in order to please you* "A hypocrite man said, `By Allah! They (hypocrites) are our chiefs and masters. If what Muhammad says is true, they are worse than donkeys.' A Muslim man heard him and declared, `By Allah! What Muhammad says is true and you are worse than a donkey!' The Muslim man conveyed what happened to the Prophet who summoned the hypocrite and asked him, *What made you say what you said?* That man invoked curses on himself and swore by Allah that he never said that. Meanwhile, the Muslim man said, `O Allah! Assert the truth of the truthful and expose the lies of the liar.' Allah revealed this Verse.'" Allah's statement, *Know they not that whoever opposes and shows hostility to Allah and His Messenger*, means, have they not come to know and realize that those who defy, oppose, wage war and reject Allah, thus becoming on one side while Allah and His Messenger on another side, *certainly for him will be the fire of Hell to abide therein*, in a humiliating torment, *That is the extreme disgrace* 9:63, that is the greatest disgrace and the tremendous misery.

Mujahid said, "The hypocrites would say something to each other then declare, `We wish that Allah does not expose this secret of ours,"

Abdullah bin `Umar said, "During the battle of Tabuk, a man was sitting in a gathering and said, `I have never seen like these reciters of ours! They have the hungriest stomachs, the most lying tongues and are the most cowardice in battle.' A man in the Masjid said, `You lie. You are a hypocrite, and I will surely inform the Messenger of Allah. ' This statement was conveyed to the Messenger of Allah and also a part of the Qur'an was revealed about it.'" `Abdullah bin `Umar said, "I have seen that man afterwards holding onto the shoulders of the Messenger's camel while stones were falling on him, declaring, `O Allah's Messenger! We were only engaged in idle talk and jesting,' while the Messenger of Allah was reciting, *"Was it at Allah, and His Ayat and His Messenger that you were mocking*'' 9:65 '" Allah said, *Make no excuse; you disbelieved after you had believed.* on account of your statement and mocking, *If We pardon some of you, We will punish others among you* for not all of you will be forgiven, some will have to taste the torment, *because they were criminals*, because of this terrible, sinful statement.

Allah admonishes the hypocrites who, unlike the believers, who enjoin righteousness and forbid evil, *they enjoin evil, and forbid the good, and they close their hands*, from spending in Allah's cause, *They have forgotten Allah*, they have forgotten the remembrance of Allah, *so He has forgotten them*, by treating them as if He has forgotten them.

O Prophet (Muhammad)! Strive hard against the disbelievers and the hypocrites, and be harsh against them, their abode is Hell, - and worst indeed is that destination. (73) They swear by Allâh that they said nothing (bad), but really they said the word of disbelief, and they disbelieved after accepting Islâm, and they resolved that (plot to murder Prophet Muhammad) which they were unable to carry out, and they could not find any cause to do so except that Allâh and His Messenger had enriched them of His Bounty. If then they repent, it will be better for them, but if they turn away, Allâh will punish them with a painful torment in this worldly life and in the Hereafter. And there is none for them on earth as a Walî (supporter, protector) or a helper. (74) And of them are some who made a covenant with Allâh (saying): "If He bestowed on us of His Bounty, we will verily, give Sadaqâh (Zakât and voluntary charity in Allâh's Cause) and will be certainly among those who are righteous." (75) Then when He gave them of His Bounty, they became niggardly [refused to pay the Sadaqâh (Zakât or voluntary charity)], and turned away, averse. (76) So He punished them by putting hypocrisy into their hearts till the Day whereon they shall meet Him, because they broke that (covenant with Allâh) which they had promised to Him and because they used to tell lies. (77) Know they not that Allâh knows their secret ideas, and their Najwa (secret counsels), and that Allâh is the All-Knower of the unseen. (78) Those who defame such of the believers who give charity (in Allâh's Cause) voluntarily, and such who could not find to give charity (in Allâh's Cause) except what is available to them, so they mock at them (believers), Allâh will throw back their mockery on them, and they shall have a painful torment.

Allah commanded His Messenger to strive hard against the disbelievers and the hypocrites and to be harsh against them. Allah also commanded him to be merciful with the believers who followed him, informing him that the destination of the disbelievers and hypocrites is the Fire in the Hereafter. Ibn Mas`ud commented on Allah's statement, *Strive hard against the disbelievers and the hypocrites* "With the hand, or at least have a stern face with them." Ibn `Abbas said, "Allah commanded the Prophet to fight the disbelievers with the sword, to strive against the hypocrites with the tongue and annulled lenient treatment of them." Ad-Dahhak commented, "Perform Jihad against the disbelievers with the sword and be harsh with the hypocrites with words, and this is the Jihad performed against them." Similar was said by Muqatil and Ar-Rabi`. Al-Hasan and Qatadah said, "Striving against them includes establishing the (Islamic Penal) Law of equality against them." In combining these statements, we could say that Allah causes punishment of the disbelievers and hypocrites with all of these methods in various conditions and situations, and Allah knows best.

Al-Amawi said in his Book on Battles, "Muhammad bin Ishaq narrated that Az-Zuhri said that `Abdur-Rahman bin `Abdullah bin Ka`b bin Malik narrated from his father, from his grandfather that he said, `Among the hypocrites who lagged behind from battle and concerning whom the Qur'an was revealed, was Al-Julas bin Suwayd bin As-Samit, who was married to the mother of `Umayr bin Sa`d. `Umayr was under the care of Al-Julas. When the Qur'an was revealed about the hypocrites, exposing their practices, Al-Julas said, `By Allah! If this man (Muhammad) is saying the truth, then we are worse than donkeys.' `Umayr bin Sa`d heard him and said, `By Allah, O Julas! You are the dearest person to me, has the most favor on me and I would hate that harm should touch you, more than I do concerning anyone else! You have uttered a statement that if I exposed, will expose you, but if I hide, it will destroy me. One of them is a lesser evil than the other.' So `Umayr went to the Messenger of Allah and told him what Al-Julas said. On realizing this, Al-Julas went to the Prophet and swore by Allah that he did not say what `Umayr bin Sa`d conveyed he said. `He lied on me,' Al-Julas said. Allah sent in his case this verse, *They swear by Allah that they said nothing (bad), but really they said the word of disbelief, and they disbelieved after accepting Islam* until the end of Ayah. The Messenger of Allah conveyed this Ayah to Al-Julas, who, they claim, repented and his repentance was sincere, prompting him to refrain from hypocrisy.'"

Imam Abu Ja`far Ibn Jarir recorded that Ibn `Abbas said, "The Messenger of Allah was sitting under the shade of a tree when he said, *A man will now come and will look to you through the eyes of a devil. When he comes, do not talk to him.*' A man who looked as if he was blue (so dark) came and the Messenger of Allah summoned him and said, *Why do you curse me, you and your companions* That man went and brought his friends and they swore by Allah that they did nothing of the sort, and the Prophet pardoned them. Allah, the Exalted and Most Honored revealed this verse, *They swear by Allah that they said nothing (bad)*...

Allah said next, *and they resolved that which they were unable to carry out* It was said that this Ayah was revealed about Al-Julas bin Suwayd, who tried to kill his wife's son when he said he would inform the Messenger of Allah about Al-Julas' statement we mentioned earlier. It was also said that it was revealed in the case of `Abdullah bin Ubayy who plotted to kill the Messenger of Allah . As-Suddi said, "This verse was revealed about some men who wanted to crown `Abdullah bin Ubayy even if the Messenger of Allah did not agree. It was reported that some hypocrites plotted to kill the Prophet, while he was at the battle of Tabuk, riding one night. They were a group of more than ten men. Ad-Dahhak said, "This Ayah was revealed about them." In his book, Dala'il An-Nubuwah, Al-Hafiz Abu Bakr Al-Bayhaqi recorded that Hudhayfah bin Al-Yaman said, "I was holding the bridle of the Messenger's camel while `Ammar was leading it, or vise versa. When we reached Al-`Aqabah, twelve riders intercepted the Prophet . When I alerted the Messenger , he shouted at them and they all ran away. The Messenger of Allah asked us, *Did you know who they were We said, `No, O Allah's Messenger! They had masks. However, we know their horses.' He said, They are the hypocrites until the Day of Resurrection. Do you know what they intended? We said, `No.' He said, They wanted to mingle with the Messenger of Allah and throw him from the `Aqabah (to the valley). We said, `O Allah's Messenger! Should you ask their tribes to send the head of each one of them to you' He said, No, for I hate that the Arabs should say* that Muhammad used some people in fighting and when Allah gave him victory with their help, he commanded that they be killed. He then said, O Allah! Throw the Dubaylah at them. We asked, `What is the Dubaylah, O Allah's Messenger' He said, A missile of fire that falls on the heart of one of them and brings about his demise." Abu At-Tufayl said, "Once, there was a dispute between Hudhayfah and another man, who asked him, `I ask you by Allah, how many were the Companions of Al-`Aqabah' The people said to Hudhayfah, `Tell him, for he asked you.' Hudhayfah said, `We were told that they were fourteen men, unless you were one of them, then the number is fifteen! I testify by Allah that twelve of them are at war with Allah and His Messenger in this life and when the witness comes forth for witness. Three of them were pardoned, for they said, `We did not hear the person whom the Messenger sent to announce something, and we did not know what the people had plotted,' for the Prophet had been walking when he said, *Water is scarce, so none among you should reach it before me.* When he found that some people had reached it before him, he cursed them.'" `Ammar bin Yasir narrated in a Hadith collected by Muslim, that Hudhayfah said to him that the Prophet said, *Among my Companions are twelve hypocrites who will never enter Paradise or find its scent, until the camel enters the thread of the needle. Eight of them will be struck by the Dubaylah, which is a missile made of fire that appears between their shoulders and pierces their chest.* This is why Hudhayfah was called the holder of the secret, for he knew who these hypocrites were, since the Messenger of Allah gave their names to him and none else.

Allah said next, *and they could not find any cause to do so except that Allah and His Messenger had enriched them of His bounty.* This Ayah means, the Messenger did not commit an error against them, other than that Allah has enriched them on account of the Prophet's blessed and honorable mission! And had Allah guided them to what the Prophet came with, they would have experienced its delight completely. The Prophet once said to the Ansar, *Have I not found you misguided and Allah guided you through me, divided and Allah united you through me, and poor and Allah enriched you through me* Whenever the Messenger asked them a question, they replied, "Allah and His Messenger have granted the favor." This type of statement, *And they had no fault except that they believed in Allah...,* is uttered when there is no wrong committed. Allah called the hypocrites to repent, *If then they repent, it will be better for them, but if they turn away; Allah will punish them with a painful torment in this worldly life and in the Hereafter.* The Ayah says, if they persist on their ways, Allah will inflict a painful torment on them in this life, by killing, sadness and depression, and in the Hereafter with torment, punishment, disgrace and humiliation, *And there is none for them on earth as a protector or a helper.* who will bring to them happiness, aid them, bring about benefit or fend off harm.

Allah says, some hypocrites give Allah their strongest oaths that if He enriches them from His bounty, they will give away alms and be among the righteous. However, they did not fulfill their vows or say the truth with their words. The consequence of this action is that hypocrisy was placed in their hearts until the Day they meet Allah the Exalted, on the

Day of Resurrection. We seek refuge with Allah from such an end. Allah states that He knows the secret and what is more hidden than the secret. He has full knowledge of what is in their hearts, even when they pretend that they will give away alms, if they acquire wealth, and will be grateful to Allah for it. Truly, Allah knows them better than they know themselves, for He is the All-Knower of all unseen and apparent things, every secret, every session of counsel, and all that is seen and hidden.

Among the traits of the hypocrites is that they will not leave anyone without defaming and ridiculing him in all circumstances even those who give away charity. If, for instance, someone gives away a large amount, the hypocrites say that he is showing off. If someone gives away a small amount they say that Allah stands not in need of this man's charity. Al-Bukhari recorded that `Ubaydullah bin Sa`id said that Abu An-Nu`man Al-Basri said that Shu`bah narrated that Sulayman said that Abu Wa'il said that Abu Mas`ud said, "When the verses of charity were revealed, we used to work as porters. A man came and distributed objects of charity in abundance and they (hypocrites) said, `He is showing off.' Another man came and gave a Sa` (a small measure of food grains); they said, `Allah is not in need of this small amount of charity.' Then the Ayah was revealed; *Those who defame those who of the believers who give charity...*" Muslim collected this Hadith in the Sahih.

Al-`Awfi narrated that Ibn `Abbas said, "One day, the Messenger of Allah went out to the people and called them to bring forth their charity, and they started bringing their charity. Among the last to come forth was a man who brought a Sa` of dates, saying, `O Allah's Messenger! This is a Sa` of dates. I spent the night bringing water and earned two Sa` of dates for my work. I kept one Sa` and brought you the other Sa`. ' The Messenger of Allah ordered him to add it to the charity. Some men mocked that man, saying, `Allah and His Messenger are not in need of this charity. What benefit would this Sa` of yours bring' `Abdur-Rahman bin `Awf asked Allah's Messenger , `Are there any more people who give charity' The Messenger of Allah said, *None besides you!*`Abdur-Rahman bin `Awf said, `I will give a hundred Uqiyah of gold as a charity.' `Umar bin Al-Khattab said to him, `Are you crazy' `Abdur-Rahman said, `I am not crazy.' `Umar said, `Have you given what you said would give' `Abdur-Rahman said, `Yes. I have eight thousand (Dirhams), four thousand I give as a loan to my Lord and four thousand I keep for myself.' The Messenger of Allah said, *May Allah bless you for what you kept and what you gave away*. However, the hypocrites defamed him, `By Allah! `Abdur-Rahman gave what he gave just to show off.' They lied, for `Abdur-Rahman willingly gave that money, and Allah revealed about his innocence and the innocence of the fellow who was poor and brought only a Sa` of dates. Allah said in His Book, *Those who defame such of the believers who give charity voluntarily* 9:79.'" A similar story was narrated from Mujahid and several others. Ibn Ishaq said, "Among the believers who gave away charity were `Abdur-Rahman bin `Awf who gave four thousand Dirhams and `Asim bin

`Adi from Bani `Ajlan. This occurred after the Messenger of Allah encouraged and called for paying charity. `Abdur-Rahman bin `Awf stood and gave away four thousand Dirhams. `Asim bin `Adi also stood and gave a hundred Wasaq of dates, but some people defamed them, saying, `They are showing off.' As for the person who gave the little that he could afford, he was Abu `Aqil, from Bani Anif Al-Arashi, who was an ally of Bani `Amr bin `Awf. He brought a Sa` of dates and added it to the charity. They laughed at him, saying, `Allah does not need the Sa` of Abu `Aqil.'" Allah said, *so they mock at them (believers); Allah will throw back their mockery on them* rebuking them for their evil actions and defaming the believers. Truly, the reward, or punishment, is equitable to the action. Allah treated them the way mocked people are treated, to aid the believers in this life. Allah has prepared a painful torment in the Hereafter for the hypocrites, for the recompense is similar to the deed.

9:81-87

Those who stayed away (from Tabuk expedition) rejoiced in their staying behind the Messenger of Allâh; they hated to strive and fight with their properties and their lives in the Cause of Allâh, and they said: "March not forth in the heat." Say: "The Fire of Hell is more intense in heat", if only they could understand! (81) So let them laugh a little and (they will) cry much as a recompense of what they used to earn (by committing sins). (82) If Allâh brings you back to a party of them (the hypocrites), and they ask your permission to go out (to fight), say: "Never shall you go out

with me, nor fight an enemy with me; you were pleased to sit
(inactive) on the first occasion, then you sit (now) with those who
lag behind." (83) And never pray (funeral prayer) for any of them
(hypocrites) who dies, nor stand at his grave. Certainly they
disbelieved in Allâh and His Messenger, and died while they were
Fâsiqûn (rebellious, - disobedient to Allâh and His Messenger).
(84) And let not their wealth or their children amaze you. Allâh's
Plan is to punish them with these things in this world, and that
their souls shall depart (die) while they are disbelievers. (85) And
when a Sûrah (chapter from the Qur'ân) is revealed, enjoining
them to believe in Allâh and to strive hard and fight along with
His Messenger, the wealthy among them ask your leave to exempt
them (from Jihâd) and say, "Leave us (behind), we would be with
those who sit (at home)." (86) They are content to be with those
(the women) who sit behind (at home). Their hearts are sealed up
(from all kinds of goodness and right guidance), so they
understand not.

Allah admonishes the hypocrites who lagged behind from
the battle of Tabuk with the Companions of the Messenger
of Allah , rejoicing that they remained behind after the
Messenger departed for the battle. The recompense of an evil
deed includes being directed to follow it with another evil deed,
while the reward of a good deed includes being directed to
another good deed after it. For instance, Allah said "...*then you sit*
(now) with those who lag behind." in reference to the men who
lagged behind from Tabuk battle, according to Ibn `Abbas.

Allah commands His Messenger to disown the hypocrites, to
abstain from praying the funeral prayer when any of them
dies, from standing next to his grave to seek Allah's

forgiveness for him, or to invoke Allah for his benefit. This is because hypocrites disbelieved in Allah and His Messenger and died as such. This ruling applies to all who are known to be hypocrites, even though it was revealed about the specific case of `Abdullah bin Ubayy bin Salul, the chief hypocrite.

Allah chastises and admonishes those who stayed away from Jihad and refrained from performing it, even though they had the supplies, means and ability to join it. They asked the Messenger for permission to stay behind, saying, *"Leave us (behind), we would be with those who sit (at home)"* thus accepting for themselves the shame of lagging behind with women, after the army had left. If war starts, such people are the most cowardice, but when it is safe, they are the most boastful among men.

9:90

And those who made excuses from the bedouins came (to you, O Prophet) asking your permission to exempt them (from the battle), and those who had lied to Allâh and His Messenger sat at home (without asking the permission for it); a painful torment will seize those of them who disbelieve.

9:94-96

They (the hypocrites) will present their excuses to you (Muslims), when you return to them. Say "Present no excuses, we shall not believe you. Allâh has already informed us of the news concerning you. Allâh and His Messenger will observe your deeds. In the end you will be brought back to the All-Knower of the unseen and the

seen, then He (Allâh) will inform you of what you used to do."
(94) They will swear by Allâh to you (Muslims) when you return
to them, that you may turn away from them. So turn away from
them. Surely, they are Rijs [i.e. Najas (impure) because of their evil
deeds], and Hell is their dwelling place, - a recompense for that
which they used to earn. (95) They (the hypocrites) swear to you
(Muslims) that you may be pleased with them, but if you are
pleased with them, certainly Allâh is not pleased with the people
who are Al-Fâsiqûn (disobedient to Allâh)

Allah said that when the believers go back to Al-Madinah,
the hypocrites will begin apologizing to them. *Say "Present*
no excuses, we shall not believe you.'', we shall not believe what
you say. Allah said that the hypocrites will swear to the
believers in apology, so that the believers turn away from
them without admonishing them. Therefore, Allah ordered
disgracing them by turning away from them, for they are,
Rijs meaning, impure inwardly and in their creed. Their
destination in the end will be Jahannam.

9:101

And among the bedouins round about you, some are hypocrites,
and so are some among the people of Al-Madinah, who persist in
hypocrisy; you (O Muhammad) know them not, We know them.
We shall punish them twice, and thereafter they shall be brought
back to a great (horrible) torment.

Allah informs His Messenger, peace be upon him, that
among the bedouins around Al-Madinah there are
hypocrites and in Al-Madinah itself. The Messenger knew

65

that some of those who associated with him from the people of Al-Madinah were hypocrites, and he used to see them day and night but did not know who they were exactly. `Abdur-Razzaq narrated that Ma`mar said that Qatadah commented on this Ayah 9:101 "What is the matter with some people who claim to have knowledge about other people, saying, `So-and-so is in Paradise and so-and-so is in the Fire.' If you ask any of these people about himself, he would say, `I do not know (if I will end up in Paradise or the Fire)!' Verily, you have more knowledge of yourself than other people. You have assumed a job that even the Prophets before you refrained from assuming.

Mujahid said about Allah's statement, *We shall punish them twice*, "By killing and capture." In another narration he said, "By hunger and torment in the grave, *and thereafter they shall be brought back to a great (horrible) torment*." `Abdur-Rahman bin Zayd bin Aslam said, "The torment in this life strikes their wealth and offspring," and he recited this Ayah *So let not their wealth nor their children amaze you; Allah only wants to punish them with these things in the life of this world.* 9:55 These afflictions torment them, but will bring reward for the believers. As for the torment in the Hereafter, it is in the Fire.

9:107-110

And as for those who put up a mosque by way of harm and disbelief, and to disunite the believers, and as an outpost for those who warred against Allâh and His Messenger (Muhammad) aforetime, they will indeed swear that their intention is nothing

but good. Allâh bears witness that they are certainly liars. (107)
Never stand you therein. Verily, the mosque whose foundation was
laid from the first day on piety is more worthy that you stand
therein (to pray). In it are men who love to clean and to purify
themselves. And Allâh loves those who make themselves clean and
pure (i.e. who clean their private parts with dust [which has the
cleansing properties of soap) and water from urine and stools, after
answering the call of nature]. (108) Is it then he who laid the
foundation of his building on piety to Allâh and His Good Pleasure
better, or he who laid the foundation of his building on the brink of
an undetermined precipice ready to crumble down, so that it
crumbled to pieces with him into the Fire of Hell. And Allâh
guides not the people who are the Zâlimûn (cruel, violent, proud,
polytheist and wrong-doer). (109) The building which they built
will never cease to be a cause of hypocrisy and doubt in their
hearts, unless their hearts are cut to pieces. (i.e. till they die). And
Allâh is All-Knowing, All-Wise.

The reason behind revealing these honorable Ayat is that
before the Messenger of Allah migrated to Al-Madinah,
there was a man from Al-Khazraj called "Abu `Amir Ar-
Rahib (the Monk)." This man embraced Christianity before
Islam and read the Scriptures. During the time of Jahiliyyah,
Abu `Amir was known for being a worshipper and being a
notable person among Al-Khazraj. When the Messenger of
Allah arrived at Al-Madinah after the Hijrah, the Muslims
gathered around him and the word of Islam was triumphant
on the day of Badr, causing Abu `Amir, the cursed one, to
choke on his own saliva and announce his enmity to Islam.
He fled from Al-Madinah to the idolators of Quraysh in

Makkah to support them in the war against the Messenger of Allah . The Quraysh united their forces and the bedouins who joined them for the battle of Uhud, during which Allah tested the Muslims, but the good end is always for the pious and righteous people. The rebellious Abu `Amir dug many holes in the ground between the two camps, into one of which the Messenger fell, injuring his face and breaking one of his right lower teeth. He also sustained a head injury. Before the fighting started, Abu `Amir approached his people among the Ansar and tried to convince them to support and agree with him. When they recognized him, they said, "May Allah never burden an eye by seeing you, O Fasiq one, O enemy of Allah!" They cursed him and he went back declaring, "By Allah! Evil has touched my people after I left." The Messenger of Allah called Abu `Amir to Allah and recited the Qur'an to him before his flight to Makkah, but he refused to embrace Islam and rebelled. The Messenger invoked Allah that Abu `Amir die as an outcast in an alien land, and his invocation came true. After the battle of Uhud was finished, Abu `Amir realized that the Messenger's call was still rising and gaining momentum, so he went to Heraclius, the emperor of Rome, asking for his aid against the Prophet . Heraclius gave him promises and Abu `Amir remained with him. He also wrote to several of his people in Al-Madinah, who embraced hypocrisy, promising and insinuating to them that he will lead an army to fight the Messenger of Allah to defeat him and his call. He ordered them to establish a stronghold where he could send his emissaries and to serve as an outpost when he joins them later on. These hypocrites built a Masjid next to the Masjid in Quba', and they finished building it before the Messenger went to Tabuk. They went to the Messenger inviting him to pray in their Masjid so that it would be a proof that the Messenger approved of their Masjid. They told him that they built the Masjid for the weak and ill persons on rainy nights. However, Allah prevented His Messenger from praying in that Masjid. He said to them, *If we come back from our travel, Allah willing*." When the Messenger of Allah came back from Tabuk and was approximately one or two days away from Al-Madinah, Jibril came down to him with the news about Masjid Ad-Dirar and the disbelief and division between the believers, who were in Masjid Quba' (which was built on piety from the first day), that Masjid Ad-Dirar was meant to achieve. Therefore, the Messenger of Allah sent some people to Masjid Ad-Dirar to bring it down before he reached Al-Madinah. `Ali bin Abi Talhah reported that Ibn `Abbas said about this Ayah (9:107), "They are some people of the Ansar to whom Abu `Amir said, `Build a Masjid and prepare whatever you can of power and weapons, for I am headed towards Caesar, emperor of Rome, to bring Roman soldiers with whom I will expel Muhammad and his companions.' When they built their Masjid, they went to the Prophet and said to him, "We finished building our Masjid and we would like you pray in it and invoke Allah for us for His blessings."

After the revelation of these ayah it was decided by the Prophet to demolish this place of mischief so they can no longer make plans to attack the Muslims.

Tabari reported: "The Messenger of God proceeded until he halted in Dhu Awan, a town an hour's daytime journey from Medina. The people who had built the Mosque of dissent (Masjid al-Dirar) had come to him while he was preparing for Tabuk, saying, 'O Messenger of God, we have built a mosque for the sick and needy and for rainy and cold nights, and we would like you to visit us and pray for us in it.' [The Prophet] said that he was on the verge of travelling, and was preoccupied, or words to that effect, and that when he returned, God willing, he would come to them and pray for them in it. When he stopped in Dhu Awan, news of the mosque came to him, and he summoned Malik b. Dukhshum, a brother of the Banu Salim, b. Awf, and Ma'n b. Adi, or his brother Asim b. Adi, brothers of the Banu al-Ajlan, and said, 'Go to this mosque whose owners are unjust people and destroy and burn it.' They went out briskly until they came to the Banu Salim b. Awf who were malik b. Al-Dukhsum's clan. Malik said to Ma'n, 'Wait for me until I bring fire from my people.' He went to his kinsfolk and took a palm branch and lighted it. Then both of them ran until they entered the mosque, its people inside, set fire to it and destroyed it and the people dispersed.

These ayat encourages praying in Masjids that were built for the purpose of worshipping Allah alone, without partners. It is also recommended to join the prayer with the believing group and worshippers who implement their faith, those who perform Wudu' perfectly and preserve themselves from impure things.

9:124-127

And whenever there comes down a Sûrah (chapter from the Qur'ân), some of them (hypocrites) say: "Which of you has had his Faith increased by it?" As for those who believe, it has increased their Faith, and they rejoice. (124) But as for those in whose hearts is a disease (of doubt, disbelief and hypocrisy), it will add suspicion and doubt to their suspicion, disbelief and doubt, and they die while they are disbelievers. (125) See they not that they are put in trial once or twice every year (with different kinds of calamities, disease, famine)? Yet, they turn not in repentance, nor do they learn a lesson (from it). (126) And whenever there comes down a Sûrah (chapter from the Qur'ân), they look at one another (saying): "Does any one see you?" Then they turn away. Allâh has turned their hearts (from the light) because they are a people that understand not.

Ayah 9:124 is one of the mightiest evidences that faith increases and decreases, as is the belief of most of the Salaf and later generations of scholars and Imams. Many scholars said that there is a consensus on this ruling. Mujahid said that hypocrites are tested with drought and hunger. This ayah perfectly describes the hypocrites in this life, for they do not remain where the truth is being declared, neither accepting nor understanding it. They neither understand Allah's Word nor attempt to comprehend it nor want it. Rather, they are too busy, turning away from it. This is why they ended up in this condition.

19:59

Then, there has succeeded them a posterity who have given up As-Salât (the prayers) [i.e. made their Salât (prayers) to be lost, either by not offering them or by not offering them perfectly or by not offering them in their proper fixed times] and have followed lusts. So they will be thrown in Hell.

Losing their prayers is when they do not consider the prayers obligatory. Therefore they lose, because the prayer is the pillar and foundation of the religion. It is the best of the servants' deeds. Thus, these people will occupy themselves with worldly desires and delights, and they will be pleased with the life of this world. They will be tranquil and at ease in the worldly appetites. Therefore, these people will meet with Ghaiy, which means loss on the Day of Resurrection. Al-Awza`i reported from Musa bin Sulayman, who reported from Al-Qasim bin Mukhaymirah that he said concerning Allah's statement, *Then, there has succeeded them a posterity who have lost the Salah* "This means that they will not keep up with the proper times of the prayer, because if it meant complete abandonment of the prayer, this would be disbelief." Masruq said, "No one who guards the five daily prayers will be written among the heedless. In their neglect is destruction. Their neglect is delaying them past their fixed times." Al-Awza`i reported from Ibrahim bin Zayd that Umar bin `Abdul-`Aziz recited the Ayah, *Then, there has succeeded them a posterity who have lost the Salah and have followed lusts. So they will meet Ghayy.* Then, he said, "Their loss was not their abandonment of the prayers, but it was by not offering them during their proper and prescribed times."

And among mankind is he who worships Allâh as it were, upon the edge (i.e. in doubt); if good befalls him, he is content therewith; but if a trial befalls him, he turns back on his face (i.e. reverts back to disbelief after embracing Islâm). He loses both this world and the Hereafter. That is the evident loss. (11) He calls besides Allâh unto that which hurts him not, nor profits him. That is a straying far away. (12) He calls unto him whose harm is nearer than his profit; certainly, an evil Maula (patron) and certainly an evil friend!

Mujahid, Qatadah and others said: *upon the edge* means, in doubt. Others said that it meant on the edge, such as on the edge or side of a mountain, i.e., (this person) enters Islam on the edge, and if he finds what he likes he will continue, otherwise he will leave. Al-Bukhari recorded that Ibn `Abbas said: *And among mankind is he who worships Allah as it were upon the edge.* "People would come to Al-Madinah to declare their Islam and if their wives gave birth to sons and their mares gave birth to foals, they would say, `This is a good religion,' but if their wives and their mares did not give birth, they would say, `This is a bad religion.'" Al-`Awfi reported that Ibn `Abbas said, "One of them would come to Al-Madinah, which was a land that was infected with a contagious disease. If he remained healthy there, and his mare foaled and his wife gave birth to a boy, he would be content, and would say, `I have not experienced anything but good since I started to follow this religion." *but if a Fitnah strikes him,* Fitnah here means affliction, i.e., if the disease of Al-Madinah befalls him, and his wife gives birth to a girl and charity is delayed in coming to him, the Shaytan comes to him and says: `By Allah, since you started to follow this religion of yours, you have experienced nothing but bad things,' and this is the Fitnah." This was also mentioned by Qatadah, Ad-Dahhak, Ibn Jurayj and others among the Salaf.

24:47-50

They (hypocrites) say: "We have believed in Allâh and in the Messenger (Muhammad), and we obey," then a party of them turn away thereafter, such are not believers. (47) And when they are called to Allâh (i.e. His Words, the Qur'ân) and His Messenger, to judge between them, lo! a party of them refuse (to come) and turn away. (48) But if the truth is on their sides, they come to him willingly with submission. (49) Is there a disease in their hearts? Or do they doubt or fear lest Allâh and His Messenger should wrong them in judgement. Nay, it is they themselves who are the Zâlimûn (polytheists, hypocrites and wrong-doers).

Allah tells us about the characteristics of the hypocrites who show one thing while hiding another, and who say with their tongues, *"We have believed in Allah and in the Messenger, and we obey,"* then a party of them turn away thereafter, meaning, their actions contradict their deeds, and they say that which they do not do. Allah says: *such are not believers.*

And when they are called to Allah and His Messenger, to judge between them... means, when they are asked to follow the guidance which Allah has revealed to His Messenger , they turn away and are too arrogantly proud of themselves to follow him.

But if the truth is on their side, they come to him willingly with submission. means, if the ruling will be in their favor and not against them, then they will come and will listen and obey, which is what is meant by the phrase *willingly with submission.* But if the ruling will go against him, he turns away and demands something that goes against the truth, and he prefers to refer for judgement to someone other than the Prophet so that his false claims may prevail. His acceptance in the beginning was not because he believed that it was the truth, but because it happened to be in accordance with his desires. So when the truth went against what he was hoping for, he turned away from it. Allah said: *Is there a disease in their hearts...* meaning, their situation cannot be anything else, they must necessarily have a disease in their hearts, or else they have some doubts about the religion, or they are afraid that Allah and His Messenger will be unjust in their ruling against them. Whichever it is, it is pure disbelief, and Allah knows which of these characteristics each one of them has.

24:53

They swear by Allâh their strongest oaths, that if only you would order them, they would leave (their homes for fighting in Allâh's Cause). Say: "Swear you not; (this) obedience (of yours) is known (to be false). Verily, Allâh knows well what you do."

It was said that the meaning is, your obedience is known, i.e., it is known that your obedience is merely verbal and is

75

not accompanied by action. Every time you swear an oath you lie.

29:10-11

Of mankind are some who say: "We believe in Allâh," but if they are made to suffer for the sake of Allâh, they consider the trial of mankind as Allâh's punishment, and if victory comes from your Lord, (the hypocrites) will say: "Verily! We were with you (helping you)." Is not Allâh Best Aware of what is in the breast of the 'Alamîn (mankind and jinn). (10) Verily, Allâh knows those who believe, and verily, He knows the hypocrites [Allâh will test the people with good and hard days to discriminate the good from the wicked although Allâh knows all before putting them to test)].

Allah mentions the descriptions of the liars who falsely claim faith with their lips, while faith is not firm in their hearts. When a test or trial comes in this world, they think that this is a punishment from Allah, so they leave Islam. Allah says: *Of mankind are some who say: "We believe in Allah."* *But if they are made to suffer for Allah, they consider the trial of mankind as Allah's punishment*; Ibn `Abbas said, "Meaning that their trial is leaving Islam if they are made to suffer for Allah." This was also the view of others among the Salaf. Allah will test the people with calamities and with times of ease, so that He may distinguish the believers from the hypocrites, to see who will obey Allah both in times of hardship and of ease, and who will obey Him only when things are going in accordance with their desires.

33:1

O Prophet (Muhammad)! Keep your duty to Allâh, and obey not the disbelievers and the hypocrites (i.e., do not follow their advice). Verily, Allâh is Ever All¬Knower, All¬Wise.

Here Allah points out something lower by referring to something higher. When He commands His servant and Messenger to do this, He is also commanding those who are lower than him, and the command is addressed to them more so. Talq bin Habib said: "Taqwa means obeying Allah in the light of the guidance of Allah and in hope of earning the reward of Allah, and refraining from disobeying Allah in the light of the guidance of Allah and fearing the punishment of Allah."

and obey not the disbelievers and the hypocrites. means, do not listen to what they say and do not consult them.

33:12-14

And when the hypocrites and those in whose hearts is a disease (of doubts) said: "Allâh and His Messenger promised us nothing but delusion!" (12) And when a party of them said: "O people of Yathrib (Al¬Madinah)! There is no stand (possible) for you (against the enemy attack!) Therefore go back!" And a band of them ask for permission of the Prophet saying: "Truly, our homes lie open (to the enemy)." And they lay not open. They but wished to flee. (13) And if the enemy had entered from all sides (of the city), and they had been exhorted to Al¬Fitnah (i.e. to renegade from Islâm to polytheism) they would surely have committed it and would have hesitated thereupon but little.

Allah tells us what happened when the Confederates surrounded Al-Madinah and the Muslims were besieged and found themselves in straitened circumstances, with the Messenger of Allah in their midst. They were tried and tested, and were shaken with a mighty shaking. At this time hypocrisy emerged, and those in whose hearts was a disease spoke about what they really felt. Their hypocrisy became apparent, while the one in whose heart was doubt became weak, and he expressed the ideas that were in his heart because of the weakness of his faith and the difficulty of the situation. Al-`Awfi reported that Ibn `Abbas said, "These were Banu Harithah, who said, `We fear for our homes, that they may be robbed.'" This was also stated by others. Ibn Ishaq mentioned that the one who said this was `Aws bin Qayzi. They used as an excuse to go back to their houses the claim that they were lying open and had nothing to protect them from the enemy, so they were afraid for their homes.

33:18-20

Allâh already knows those among you who keep back (men) from fighting in Allâh's Cause, and those who say to their brethren "Come here towards us," while they (themselves) come not to the battle except a little. (18) Being miserly towards you (as regards help and aid in Allâh's Cause). Then when fear comes, you will see them looking to you, their eyes revolving like (those of) one over whom hovers death, but when the fear departs, they will smite you with sharp tongues, miserly towards (spending anything in any) good (and only covetous of booty and wealth). Such have not believed. Therefore Allâh makes their deeds fruitless, and that is ever easy for Allâh. (19) They think that Al¬Ahzâb (the Confederates) have not yet withdrawn, and if Al¬Ahzâb (the Confederates) should come (again), they would wish they were in the deserts (wandering) among the bedouins, seeking news about you (from a far place); and if they (happen) to be among you, they would not fight but little.

Qatadah said: "But when it comes to the booty, the most miserly of people and the worst to have to share the booty with are those who say, `Give us, give us, we were there with you,' but during battle they were the most cowardly and the most likely to fail to support the truth." They are miserly towards good, meaning there is no goodness in them, they combined cowardice with lies and little good.

33:60

If the hypocrites, and those in whose hearts is a disease (evil desire for adultery), and those who spread false news among the people in Al¬Madinah, stop not, We shall certainly let you overpower them; then they will not be able to stay in it as your neighbours but a little while.

Allah issues a warning to the hypocrites, those who make an outward display of faith while concealing their disbelief, *those in whose hearts is a disease,* `Ikrimah and others said that this refers to adulterers in this instance. *and those who spread false news among the people in Al-Madinah* means, those who say that the enemy has come and war has started, which is a lie and a fabrication. Unless they give up these actions and return to the truth, *We shall certainly let you overpower them,*

`Ali bin Abi Talhah reported that Ibn `Abbas said, "We will give you power over them." Qatadah said: "We will incite you against them." As-Suddi said: "We will inform you about them."

47:20-26

Those who believe say: "Why is not a Sûrah (chapter of the Qur'ân) sent down (for us)? But when a decisive Sûrah (explaining and ordering things) is sent down, and fighting (Jihâd in Allâh's Cause) is mentioned (i.e. ordained) therein, you will see those in whose hearts is a disease (of hypocrisy) looking at you with a look of one fainting to death. But it was better for them (hypocrites, to listen to Allâh and to obey Him). (20) Obedience (to Allâh) and good words (were better for them). And when the matter (preparation for Jihâd) is resolved on, then if they had been true to Allâh, it would have been better for them, (21) Would you then, if you were given the authority, do mischief in the land, and sever your ties of kinship? (22) Such are they whom Allâh has cursed, so that He has made them deaf and blinded their sight. (23) Do they not then think deeply in the Qur'ân, or are their hearts locked up (from understanding it)? (24) Verily, those who have turned back (have apostatise) as disbelievers after the guidance has been manifested to them — Shaitân (Satan) has beautified for them (their false hopes), and (Allâh) prolonged their term (age). (25) This is because they said to those who hate what Allâh has sent down: "We will obey you in part of the matter," but Allâh knows their secrets.

Allah mentions that the believers were hoping that Jihad would be legislated. But when Allah ordained it, many of the people turned back, as Allah says, *Those who believe say: "Why is not a Surah sent down (for us)"* means, a Surah containing an order to fight. Then He says, *But now that a decisive Surah is sent down mentioning fighting, you can see those in whose hearts is disease looking at you with the look of one who is about to faint for fear of death.* meaning, due to their fear, terror, and cowardice concerning meeting the enemies.

Such are the ones whom Allah has cursed, so He has made them deaf and blinded their vision. This involves a general prohibition of spreading corruption on earth, and a specific prohibition of severing the ties of kinship. In fact, Allah has commanded the people to establish righteousness on earth, as well as to join the ties of kinship by treating the relatives well in speech, actions, and spending wealth in charity. Many authentic and sound Hadiths have been reported through numerous routes of transmission from Allah's Messenger in this regard. Al-Bukhari recorded from Abu Hurayrah, that Allah's Messenger said, *After Allah completed creating the creation, the womb stood up and pulled at the lower garment of the Most Merciful. He said, 'Stop that!' It replied, 'My stand here is the stand of one seeking refuge in you from severance of ties.' Allah said, 'Would it not please you that I join whoever joins you and sever whoever severs you' It replied, 'Yes indeed!' He said, 'You are granted that!'*

Imam Ahmad recorded from Abu Bakrah, may Allah be pleased with him, that Allah's Messenger said: *No sin deserves that Allah hasten its punishment in the worldly life, in addition to what He reserves in the Hereafter for those who commit it, more than injustice and severance of the ties of kinship.* This was also recorded by Abu Dawud, At-Tirmidhi, and Ibn Majah. At-Tirmidhi said, "This Hadith is Sahih."

Commanding the people to reflect and ponder upon the Qur'an, and prohibiting them from turning away from it, Allah says, *Will they not then reflect upon the Qur'an, or are there locks upon their hearts* means, there indeed are locks upon some hearts, firmly closing them so that none of its meanings can reach them. Ibn Jarir recorded from Hisham bin `Urwah, from his father, that Allah's Messenger once recited this Ayah, *Will they not then reflect upon the Qur'an, or are there locks upon their hearts* and a young man from Yemen said, "Indeed, there are locks upon them -- until Allah opens them totally or slightly." After that `Umar, always liked that young man, and kept that to himself until he became in charge, upon which he utilized him (as a consultant).

That is because they said to those who hate what Allah sent down: "We will obey you in part of the matter." means, they plotted secretly with them and gave them evil advice -- as is the common practice of the hypocrites who declare the opposite of what they conceal. Because of this, Allah says, *And Allah knows their secrets.* whatever they hide and conceal, Allah is well-acquainted with it and He knows it.

47:29-30

Or do those in whose hearts is a disease (of hypocrisy), think that Allâh will not bring to light all their hidden ill-wills? (29) Had We willed, We could have shown them to you, and you should have known them by their marks; but surely, you will know them by the tone of their speech! And Allâh knows (all) your deeds.

Or do those in whose hearts is disease think that Allah would never expose their ill--wills meaning, do the hypocrites think that Allah will not expose their affair to His believing servant? Yes indeed, He will expose their affair and manifest it so that those with insight will be able to understand it.

Had We so willed, We could have shown them clearly to you, so that you would know them by their marks. Allah is telling His Messenger , "Had We willed, O Muhammad, We would have shown you the specific individuals who are hypocrites, so that you would plainly know them." However, Allah did not do that in regard to all of the hypocrites. He conceals His creation, lets their affairs run according to apparent purity, and leaves the inner secrets to the One Who is well aware of them. Allah then adds, *But you will know them by the tone of their speech!* which means, `you will know them by their speech that reveals their intentions.' A person declares his association through the context and meaning of his words -- as the Commander of the faithful `Uthman bin `Affan, said, *"Never would one conceal a secret but Allah will expose it by the look on his face and the uncontrolled words of his tongue."*

48:6

And that He may punish the Munâfiqûn (hypocrites), men and women, and also the Mushrikûn men and women, who think evil thoughts about Allâh, for them is a disgraceful torment, And the

Anger of Allâh is upon them, and He has cursed them and prepared Hell for them — and worst indeed is that destination.

48:10-12

Verily, those who give Bai'âh (pledge) to you (O Muhammad) they are giving Bai'âh (pledge) to Allâh. The Hand of Allâh is over their hands. Then whosoever breaks his pledge, breaks it only to his own harm, and whosoever fulfils what he has covenanted with Allâh, He will bestow on him a great reward. (10) Those of the bedouins who lagged behind will say to you: "Our possessions and our families occupied us, so ask forgiveness for us." They say with their tongues what is not in their hearts. Say: "Who then has any power at all (to intervene) on your behalf with Allâh, if He intends you hurt or intends you benefit? Nay, but Allâh is Ever All-Aware of what you do. (11) "Nay, but you thought that the Messenger and the believers would never return to their families; and that was made fair-seeming in your hearts, and you did think an evil thought and you became a useless people going for destruction."

The pledge mentioned here is the pledge of Ar-Ridwan which was pledged under a tree, a Samurah, in the area of Al-Hudaybiyyah. The number of the Companions who gave their pledge to Allah's Messenger at that time was either 1,300, 1,400 or 1,500. However, 1,400 is the better choice.

Allah informs His Messenger of the excuses that the bedouins who lagged behind would offer him, those bedouins who preferred to remain in their homes and possessions and did not join the Messenger of Allah . They offered an excuse for lagging behind, as that of being busy --

in their homes and with their wealth! They asked the Messenger of Allah to invoke Allah to forgive them, not because they had faith in the Prophet and his invocation, but to show off and pretend. This is why Allah the Exalted said about them, *They say with their tongues what is not in their hearts. Say: "Who then has any power at all (to intervene) on your behalf with Allah, if He intends you hurt or intends you benefit''* Allah says, none can resist what Allah has decided in your case, all praise and honor belong to Him. Allah is the Knower of your secrets and what your hearts conceal, even if you pretend and choose to be hypocritical with us.

This is why Allah the Exalted said, *Nay, but Allah is Ever All-Aware of what you do.* then He said, *Nay, but you thought that the Messenger and the believers would never return to their families,* `for your lagging behind was not an excusable act or just a sin. Rather, your lagging behind was because of hypocrisy and because you thought that the Muslims would be killed to the extent of extermination, their lives would be extinguished and none of them will ever come back,' *and you did think an evil thought and you became a people Bur* going for destruction, according to `Abdullah bin `Abbas, Mujahid and several others. Qatadah explained Bur to mean, corrupt and some said that it is a word used in the Arabic dialect of the area of Oman. Whoever does not purify his actions outwardly and inwardly for Allah's sake, then Allah the Exalted will punish him in the Blazing Fire, even if he pretends to show people that he follows the faith, contradicting his true creed.

48:15

Those who lagged behind will say, when you set forth to take the spoils, "Allow us to follow you," They want to change Allâh's Words. Say: "You shall not follow us; thus Allâh has said beforehand." Then they will say: "Nay, you envy us." Nay, but they understand not except a little.

Allah characterizes the bedouins who lagged behind the Messenger of Allah during the `Umrah of Hudaybiyyah, saying that when the Prophet and his Companions later went on to conquer Khaybar, the bedouins asked them to take them along. They were hoping to collect war booty, having been absent when it was time to fight the enemy and enduring with patience therein. Allah the Exalted ordered His Messenger to refuse to give them permission to accompany him, being a punishment that is similar to their error. Allah has promised those who were present at Al-Hudaybiyyah to earn Khaybar's war spoils alone, not shared in that with the bedouins who lagged behind. Therefore, the legislation that Allah gave in this regard was joined to the destiny that He decided, occurring just as He decided. Allah's statement, *They want to change Allah's Words,* which refers to the promise that Allah gave those who were present at Al-Hudaybiyyah, according to the explanation reported from Mujahid, Qatadah, Juwaybir, which Ibn Jarir preferred.

57:13-15

On the Day when the hypocrites men and women will say to the believers: "Wait for us! Let us get something from your light!" It will be said: "Go back to your rear! Then seek a light!" So a wall will be put up between them, with a gate therein. Inside it will be mercy, and outside it will be torment." (13) (The hypocrites) will call the believers: "Were we not with you?" The believers will reply: "Yes! But you led yourselves into temptations, you looked forward for our destruction; you doubted (in Faith); and you were deceived by false desires, till the Command of Allâh came to pass. And the chief deceiver (Satan) deceived you in respect of Allâh." (14) So this Day no ransom shall be taken from you (hypocrites), nor of those who disbelieved, (in the Oneness of Allâh Islâmic Monotheism). Your abode is the Fire, That is your maula (friend — proper place), and worst indeed is that destination.

Ad-Dahhak commented, "Everyone will be given a light on the Day of Resurrection. When they arrive at the Sirat, the light of the hypocrites will be extinguished. When the believers see this, they will be concerned that their light also will be extinguished, just as the light of the hypocrites was. This is when the believers will invoke Allah, `O our Lord! Perfect our light for us.'"

Allah said, *On the Day when the hypocrites men and women will say to the believers: "Wait for us! Let us get something from your light!"* Allah informs us in this Ayah of the terrible horrors, horrendous incidents and tremendous events that will take place on the Day of Resurrection in the Gathering Area. No one will be saved on that Day, except those who believed in Allah and His Messenger, obeyed Allah's commands and avoided His prohibitions. Al-`Awfi, Ad-Dahhak and others reported from Ibn `Abbas: "When the people are gathering in darkness, Allah will send light, and when the believers see the light they will march towards it. This light will be their guide from Allah to Paradise. When the hypocrites see the believers following the light, they will follow them. However, Allah will extinguish the light for the hypocrites and they will say (to the believers), *Wait for us! Let us get something from your light.* The believers will reply by saying, *Go back to your rear!* to the dark area you were in, and look for a light there!'" Allah said, *So, a wall will be put up between them, with a gate therein. Inside it will be mercy, and outside it will be torment.* Al-Hasan and Qatadah said that the wall mentioned here is located between Paradise and Hellfire.

The hypocrites will call the believers: "Were we not with you'' meaning, the hypocrites will call out to the believers saying, "Were we not with you in the life of the world, attending Friday prayers and congregational prayers Did we not stand with you on Mount `Arafah (during Hajj), participate in battle by your side and perform all types of acts of worship with you" *The believers will reply: "Yes!..."* The believers will answer the hypocrites by saying, "Yes, you were with us, *But you led yourselves into temptations, you looked forward to our destruction; and you doubted (in faith) and you were deceived by false hopes,* " Qatadah said, *you looked forward to destruction,* "Of the truth and its people." *and you doubted,* that Resurrection occurs after death, *and you were deceived by false hopes,* meaning: you said that you will be forgiven your sins; or, they say it means: this life deceived you; *till the command of Allah came to pass.* meaning: you remained on this path until death came to you, *And the deceiver deceived you in*

88

regard to Allah. `the deceiver' being Shaytan. Qatadah said, "They were deceived by Ash-Shaytan. By Allah! They remained deceived until Allah cast them into Hellfire." The meaning here is that the believers will answer the hypocrites by saying, "You were with us in bodies which were heartless and devoid of intentions. You were cast in doubt and suspicion. You were showing off for people and remembered Allah, little." Mujahid commented, "The hypocrites were with the believers in this life, marrying from among each other, yet betraying them even when they were associating with them. They were dead. They will both be given a light on the Day of Resurrection, but the light of the hypocrites will be extinguished when they reach the wall; this is when the two camps separate and part!"

58:14-18

Have you not seen those (hypocrites) who take as friends a people upon whom is the Wrath of Allâh? They are neither of you (Muslims) nor of them, and they swear to a lie while they know. (14) Allâh has prepared for them a severe torment. Evil indeed is that which they used to do. (15) They have made their oaths a screen (for their evil actions). Thus they hinder (men) from the Path of Allâh, so they shall have a humiliating torment. (16) Their children and their wealth will avail them nothing against Allâh. They will be the dwellers of the Fire, to dwell therein forever. (17) On the Day when Allâh will resurrect them all together (for their account), then they will swear to Him as they swear to you (O Muslims). And they think that they have something (to stand upon). Verily, they are liars!

Allah chastises the hypocrites for secretly aiding and supporting the disbelievers even though, in reality, they were neither with the disbelievers nor with the Muslims.

Allah said here, *Have you not seen those who take as friends a people upon whom is the wrath of Allah* referring to the Jews with whom the hypocrites were allies in secret. Allah said, *They are neither of you nor of them*, meaning, that these hypocrites are neither with the believers, nor with their allies the Jews, *and they swear to a lie while they know.* meaning, the hypocrites lie when they vow, knowing that they are lying, which is called the vow of Al-Ghamus. We seek refuge with Allah from their ways. When the hypocrites met the believers they said that they believed and when they went to the Messenger, they swore to him by Allah that they were believers. They knew that they were lying in their vow, and they knew that they did not declare their true creed. This is why Allah witnessed here that they lie in their vows and know that they are lying, even though their statement (about the Prophet being Allah's Prophet) is true in essence. Allah has prepared a painful torment for the hypocrites on account of their evil deeds, their aid and support of the disbelievers and their deceit and betrayal of the believers. The hypocrites pretended to be believers and concealed disbelief under the shield of their false oaths. Many were unaware of their true stance and were thus deceived by their oaths. Because of this, some people were hindered from the Path of Allah *so they shall have a humiliating torment.* meaning, as recompense for belittling the significance of swearing by the Mighty Name of Allah, while lying and concealing betrayal.

then they will swear to Him as they swear to you. And they think that they have something. meaning, they will swear to Allah the Exalted and Most Honored that they were following the guidance and the correct path, just as they used to swear to the believers in this worldly life. Verily, those who live following on a certain path will most likely die while on it. Thus, they will be resurrected upon their path. The hypocrites will think that their vows will help them with Allah, just as they helped with the people, who were obliged to treat them as they pretended to be, Muslim. This is why Allah said, *And they think that they have something* meaning, on account of swearing to their Lord (that they used to be believers). Allah rebukes this idea of theirs, labeling the liars.

59:11-13

Have you not observed the hypocrites who say to their friends among the people of the Scripture who disbelieve: "(By Allâh) If you are expelled, we (too) indeed will go out with you, and we shall never obey any one against you, and if you are attacked (in fight), we shall indeed help you." But Allâh is Witness, that they verily, are liars. (11) Surely, if they (the Jews) are expelled, never will they (hypocrites) go out with them, and if they are attacked, they will never help them. And (even) if they do help them, they (hypocrites) will turn their backs, and they will not be victorious. (12) Verily, you (believers in the Oneness of Allâh — Islâmic Monotheism) are more fearful in their breasts than Allâh. That is because they are a people who comprehend not (the Majesty and Power of Allâh).

Allah states that the hypocrites, `Abdullah bin Ubayy and his like, sent a messenger to Bani An-Nadir promising them help. *But Allah is Witness that they verily are liars.* meaning, the hypocrites lied when they issued this promise, because it was just words that they did not intend to fulfill. Also, what they said they would do, would never have been fulfilled by them, and this is why Allah said, *and if they are attacked, they will never help them.*

63:1-8

When the hypocrites come to you (O Muhammad), they say: "We bear witness that you are indeed the Messenger of Allâh." Allâh knows that you are indeed His Messenger and Allâh bears witness that the hypocrites are liars indeed. (1) They have made their oaths a screen (for their hypocrisy). Thus they hinder (men) from the Path of Allâh. Verily, evil is what they used to do. (2) That is because they believed, then disbelieved, therefore their hearts are sealed, so they understand not. (3) And when you look at them, their bodies please you; and when they speak, you listen to their words. They are as blocks of wood propped up. They think that every cry is against them. They are the enemies, so beware of them. May Allâh curse them! How are they denying (or deviating from) the Right Path? (4) And when it is said to them: "Come, so that the Messenger of Allâh may ask forgiveness from Allâh for you", they twist their heads, and you would see them turning away their faces in pride. (5) It is equal to them whether you (Muhammad) ask forgiveness or ask not forgiveness for them. Verily, Allâh guides not the people who are the Fâsiqîn (the rebellious, the disobedient to Allâh) (6) They are the ones who say: "Spend not on those who are with Allâh's Messenger, until they desert him." And to Allâh belong the treasures of the heavens and the earth, but the hypocrites comprehend not. (7) They (hyprocrites) say: "If we return to Al-Madinah, indeed the more honourable ('Abdûllah bin Ubai bin Salul, the chief of hyprocrites at Al¬Madinah) will expel therefrom the meaner (i.e. Allâh's Messenger)." But honour, power and glory belong to Allâh, and to His Messenger (Muhammad), and to the believers, but the hypocrites know not.

Allah the Exalted states that the hypocrites pretended to be Muslims when they went to the Prophet. In reality, they were not Muslims, but rather the opposite. This is why Allah the Exalted said, *When the hypocrites come to you, they say: "We bear witness that you are indeed the Messenger of Allah."* meaning, `when the hypocrites come to you, they announce this statement and pretend to believe in it.' Allah informs that there is no substance to their statement, and this is why He said, *Allah knows that you are indeed His Messenger*, then said, *And Allah bears witness that the hypocrites are liars indeed.* meaning, their claims, even though it is true about the Prophet. But they did not believe inwardly in what they declared outwardly, and this is why Allah declared their falsehood about their creed. Allah's statement, *They have made their oaths a screen. Thus they hinder (others) from the path of Allah.* meaning, the hypocrites shield themselves from Muslims when they falsely and sinfully swear to be what they are not in reality. Some Muslims were deceived because they did not know their falsehood, and thus, thought that they were Muslims. Some Muslims believed what hypocrites say and even imitated them in their outward behavior. However, inwardly, hypocrites seek the destruction of Islam and its people, and this is why trusting them might bring great harm to many people.

This is why Allah said next, *Thus they hinder (others) from the path of Allah. Verily, evil is what they used to do.* Allah said, *That is because they believed, and then disbelieved; therefore their hearts are sealed, so they understand not.* meaning, He has decreed them to be hypocrites because they reverted from faith to disbelief and exchanged guidance for misguidance. Therefore, Allah stamped and sealed their hearts and because of it, they cannot comprehend the guidance, nor any goodness can reach their hearts. Truly, their hearts neither understand, nor attain guidance. Allah said, *And when you look at them, their bodies please you; and when they speak, you listen to their words.* meaning, hypocrites have a graceful outer appearance and are eloquent. When one hears them speak, he will listen to their eloquent words, even though hypocrites are truly weak and feeble, full of fear, fright and cowardice. Allah's statement, *They think that every cry is against them.* means, every time an incident occurs or something frightening happens, they think that it is headed their way. This is indicative of their cowardice. They are shapes that do not have much substance, and this is why Allah said, *They are the enemies, so beware of them. May Allah curse them! How are they denying the right path* means, how they are being led astray to the misguidance, away from the guidance. Imam Ahmad recorded that Abu Hurayrah said that the Prophet said, *Hypocrites have certain signs that they are known by. Their greeting is really a curse, their food is from stealing and the war booty they collect is from theft. They shun the*

Masjid and they do not come to the prayer but at its end. They are arrogant; it is neither easy for them to blend in, nor it is easy for people to blend with them. They are like pieces of wood by night and are noisy by day.

Allah the Exalted states about the hypocrites, may Allah curse them, *And when it is said to them: "Come, so that the Messenger of Allah may ask forgiveness from Allah for you,'' they twist their heads*, meaning, they turn away, ignoring this call in arrogance, belittling what they are invited to. This is why Allah the Exalted said, *and you would see them turning away their faces in pride*. Allah punished them for this behavior, saying, *It is equal to them whether you ask forgiveness or ask not forgiveness for them, Allah will never forgive them. Verily, Allah guides not the people who are the rebellious.*

Several of the Salaf mentioned that this entire passage was revealed in the case of `Abdullah bin Ubay bin Salul, as we will soon mention, Allah willing and our trust and reliance are on Him. In his book, As-Sirah, Muhammad bin Ishaq said, "After the battle of Uhud ended, the Prophet returned to Al-Madinah. `Abdullah bin Ubay bin Salul -- as Ibn Shihab narrated to me -- would stand up every Friday, without objection from anyone because he was a chief of his people, when the Prophet would sit on the Minbar, just before he delivered the Jumu`ah Khutbah to the people. `Abdullah bin Ubay would say, `O people! This is the Messenger of Allah with you. Allah has honored us by sending him and gave you might through him. Support him, honor him and listen to and obey him.' He would then sit

95

down. So after the battle of Uhud, even after he did what he did, that is, returning to Al-Madinah with a third of the army, he stood up to say the same words. But the Muslims held on to his clothes and said to him, `Sit down, O enemy of Allah! You are not worthy to stand after you did what you did.' `Abdullah went out of the Masjid crossing people's lines and saying, `By Allah, it is as if I said something awful when I wanted to support him.' Some men from Al-Ansar met him at the gate of the Masjid and asked him what happened. He said, `I just stood up to support him and some men, his Companions, jumped at me, pulled me back and admonished me, as if what I said was an awful thing; I merely wanted to support him.' They said to him, `Woe to you! Go back so that Allah's Messenger asks Allah to forgive you.' He said, `By Allah, I do not wish that he ask Allah to forgive me.'" Qatadah and As-Suddi said, "This Ayah was revealed about `Abdullah bin Ubay. A young relative of his went to Allah's Messenger and conveyed to him an awful statement that `Abdullah said. The Messenger called `Abdullah, who swore by Allah that he did not say anything. The Ansar went to that boy and admonished him. However, Allah sent down what you hear about `Abdullah's case and Allah's enemy was told, `Go to Allah's Messenger,' but he turned his head away, saying that he will not do it." Muhammad bin Ishaq said that Muhammad bin Yahya bin Hibban, `Abdullah bin Abi Bakr and `Asim bin `Umar bin Qatadah narrated to him the story of Bani Al-Mustaliq. They said that while the Messenger of Allah was in that area, Jahjah bin Sa`id Al-Ghifari, a hired hand for `Umar, and

Sinan bin Wabr fought over the water source. Sinan called out, "O Ansar", while Al-Jahjah called, "O Muhajirin!" Zayd bin Arqam and several Ansar men were sitting with `Abdullah bin Ubay bin Salul at that time. When `Abdullah heard what happened, he said, "They are bothering us in our land. By Allah, the parable of us and these foolish Quraysh men, is the parable that goes, `Feed your dog until it becomes strong, and it will eat you.' By Allah, when we go back to Al-Madinah, the most mighty will expel the weak from it." He then addressed his people who were sitting with him, saying to them, "What have you done to yourselves You let them settle in your land and shared your wealth with them. By Allah, if you abandon them, they will have to move to another area other than yours." Zayd bin Arqam heard these words and conveyed them to Allah's Messenger. Zayd was a young boy then. `Umar bin Al-Khattab was with the Messenger and he said, "O Allah's Messenger! Order `Abbad bin Bishr to cut off his head at his neck." The Prophet replied, *What if people started saying that Muhammad kills his companions, O `Umar No. However, order the people to start the journey (back to Al-Madinah).* When `Abdullah bin Ubay bin Salul was told that his statement reached Allah's Prophet , he went to him and denied saying it. He swore by Allah that he did not utter the statement that Zayd bin Arqam conveyed. `Abdullah bin Ubay was a chief of his people and they said, "O Allah's Messenger! Maybe the young boy merely guessed and did not hear what was said correctly." Allah's Messenger started the journey at an unusual hour of the day and was met by Usayd bin Al-

Hudayr, who greeted him acknowledging his prophethood. Usayd said, "By Allah! You are about to begin the journey at an unusual time." The Prophet said, *Did not the statement of your friend, Ibn Ubay reach you He claimed that when he returns to Al-Madinah, the mighty one will expel the weak one out of it.* Usayd said, "Indeed, you are the mighty one, O Allah's Messenger, and he is the disgraced one." Usayd said, "Take it easy with him, O Allah's Messenger! By Allah, when Allah brought you to us, we were about to gather the pearls (of a crown) so that we appoint him king over us. He thinks that you have rid him of his kingship." The Messenger of Allah traveled with the people until the night fell, then the rest of the night until the beginning of the next day and then set camp with the people. He wanted to busy them from talking about what had happened. The minute people felt the ground under their feet, they went to sleep and Surat Al-Munafiqin was revealed. Al-Hafiz Abu Bakr Al-Bayhaqi recorded that Jabir bin `Abdullah said, "We were in a battle with Allah's Messenger and a man from the Emigrants kicked an Ansari man. The Ansari man called out, `O Ansar!' and the Emigrant called out, `O Emigrants!' Allah's Messenger heard that and said, *What is this call of Jahiliyyah Abandon it because it is offensive.* `Abdullah bin Ubay heard that and said, `Have they (the Emigrants) done so By Allah, if we return to Al-Madinah, surely, the more honorable will expel therefrom the meaner.' The Ansar at that time, were more numerous that the Emigrants when the Messenger of Allah came to Al-Madinah, but later on the Emigrants increased in number. When this statement reached the

Prophet , `Umar got up and said, `O Allah's Messenger! Let
me chop off the head of this hypocrite!' The Prophet said:
*Leave him, lest the people say that Muhammad kills his
companions*." Imam Ahmad, Al-Bukhari and Muslim
collected this Hadith. `Ikrimah and Ibn Zayd and others said
that when the Prophet and his Companions went back to Al-
Madinah,`Abdullah, the son of `Abdullah bin Ubay bin
Salul, remained by the gate of Al-Madinah holding his
sword. People passed by him as they returned to Al-
Madinah, and then his father came. `Abdullah, son of
`Abdullah, said to his father, "Stay where you are," and his
father asked what the matter was. His son said, "By Allah!
You will not enter through here until the Messenger of Allah
allows you to do so, for he is the honorable one and you are
the disgraced." When the Messenger of Allah came by, and
he used to be in the last lines, `Abdullah bin Ubay
complained to him about his son and his son said, "By Allah,
O Allah's Messenger! He will not enter it until you say so."
The Messenger gave his permission to `Abdullah bin Ubay
and his son said, "Enter, now that the Messenger of Allah
gave you his permission." In his Musnad, Abu Bakr
`Abdullah bin Az-Zubayr Al-Humaydi recorded from Abu
Harun Al-Madani that `Abdullah, the son of `Abdullah bin
Ubay bin Salul, said to his father, "You will never enter Al-
Madinah unless and until you say, `Allah's Messenger is the
honorable one and I am the disgraced." When the Prophet
came, `Abdullah, son of `Abdullah bin Ubay bin Salul said to
him, "O Allah's Messenger! I was told that you have decided
to have my father executed. By He Who has sent you with

Truth, I never looked straight to his face out of respect for him. But if you wish, I will bring you his head, because I would hate to see the killer of my father."

66:9

O Prophet (Muhammad)! Strive hard against the disbelievers and the hypocrites, and be severe against them; their abode will be Hell, and worst indeed is that destination.

Allah the Exalted orders His Messenger to perform Jihad against the disbelievers and hypocrites, the former with weapons and armaments and the later by establishing Allah's legislated penal code, *and be severe against them* meaning, in this life, *their abode will be Hell, and worst indeed is that destination.* that is, in the Hereafter.

68:42-44

(Remember) the Day when the Shin shall be laid bare (i.e. the Day of Resurrection) and they shall be called to prostrate themselves (to Allâh), but they (hypocrites) shall not be able to do so. (42) Their eyes will be cast down and ignominy will cover them; they used to be called to prostrate themselves (offer prayers), while they were healthy and good (in the life of the world, but they did not). (43) Then leave Me Alone with such as belie this Qur'ân. We shall punish them gradually from directions they perceive not.

Al-Bukhari recorded that Abu Sa`id Al-Khudri said that he heard the Prophet saying, *Our Lord will reveal His Shin, and every believing male and female will prostrate to Him. The only people who will remain standing are those who prostrated in the worldly life only to be seen and heard (showing off). This type of person will try to prostrate at that time, but his back will made to be one stiff plate (the bone will not bend or flex)."* This Hadith was recorded in the Two Sahihs and other books from different routes of transmission with various wordings. It is a long Hadith that is very popular. Concerning Allah's statement, *Their eyes will be cast down and ignominy will cover them;* means, in the final abode, due to their crimes and arrogance in the worldly life. Thus they will be punished with the opposite of what they did. When they were called to prostrate in the worldly life, they refused to do so even though they were healthy and secure. Therefore, they will be punished with the lack of ability to do so in the Hereafter. When the Almighty Lord makes Himself visible (before the believers), then the believers will fall down in prostration to Him, but no one of the disbelievers and hypocrites will be able to prostrate. rather, their backs will become one plate. Every time one of them attempts to prostrate, he will bow his neck but will not be able to prostrate. This is just like in the life of this world, when these people were in opposition to what the believers were doing.

Then Allah says, *Then leave Me alone with such as belie this narration.* meaning, the Qur'an. This is a severe threat which means, `leave Me alone with this person; I know about him and how I will gradually punish him and increase him in his falsehood. I am giving him respite for a while, then I will seize him with a mighty and powerful punishment.' Thus, Allah says, *We shall punish them gradually from directions they perceive not.* meaning, and they will not even be aware of it. Rather, they will believe that it is a noble blessing from Allah, but really the same matter is actually a form of humiliation (for them).

107:4-7

So woe unto those performers of Salât (prayers) (hypocrites), (4) Those who delay their Salât (prayer from their stated fixed times), (5) Those who do good deeds only to be seen (of men), (6) And prevent Al-Mâ'ûn (small kindnesses like salt, sugar, water).

(*So, woe unto those performers of Salah, those who with their Salah are Sahun.*) Ibn `Abbas and others have said, "This means the hypocrites who pray in public but do not pray in private." Thus, Allah says, *unto those performers of Salah,* They are those people who pray and adhere to the prayer, yet they are mindless of it. This may either be referring to its act entirely, as Ibn `Abbas said, or it may be referring to performing it in its stipulated time that has been legislated Islamically. This means that the person prays it completely outside of its time.

`Ata' bin Dinar said, "All praise is due to Allah, the One Who said, *with their Salah are Sahun.* and He did not say, `those who are absent minded in their prayer.'" It could also mean the first time of the prayer, which means they always delay it until the end of its time, or they usually do so. It may also refer to not fulfilling its pillars and conditions, and in the required manner. It could also mean performing it with humility and contemplation of its meanings. The wording of the Ayah comprises all of these meanings. However, whoever has any characteristic of this that we have mentioned then a portion of this Ayah applies to him. And whoever has all of these characteristics, then he has completed his share of this Ayah, and the hypocrisy of actions is fulfilled in him. This is just as is confirmed in the Two Sahihs that the Messenger of Allah said, *This is the prayer of the hypocrite, this is the prayer of the hypocrite, this is the prayer of the hypocrite. He sits watching the sun until it is between the two horns of Shaytan. Then he stands and pecks four (Rak`ahs) and he does not remember Allah (in them) except very little.* This Hadith is describing the end of the time for the `Asr prayer, which is the middle prayer as is confirmed by a text (Hadith). This is the time in which it is disliked to pray. Then this person stands to pray it, pecking in it like the pecking of a crow. He does not have tranquility or humility in it at all. Thus, the Prophet said, *He does not remember Allah (in them) except very little.* He probably only stands to pray it so that the people will see him praying, and not seeking the Face of Allah. This is just as if he did not pray at all. Allah says, *Verily, the hypocrites seek to deceive Allah, but it is He Who deceives them. And when they stand up with laziness and to be seen of men, and they do not remember Allah but little.* (4:142) and Allah says here, *Those who do good deeds only to be seen,* Imam Ahmad recorded from `Amr bin Murrah that he said, "We were sitting with Abu `Ubaydah when the people mentioned showing-off. A man known as Abu Yazid said, "I heard `Abdullah bin `Amr saying that the Messenger of Allah said, *Whoever tries to make the people hear of his deed,*

103

Allah, the One Who hears His creation, will hear it and make him despised and degraded." from what is related to his statement,

Those who do good deeds only to be seen. is that whoever does a deed solely for Allah, but the people come to know about it, and he is pleased with that, then this is not considered showing off. Allah said: *And withhold Al-Ma`un.* This means that they do not worship their Lord well, nor do they treat His creation well. They do not even lend that which others may benefit from and be helped by, even though the object will remain intact and be returned to them. These people are even stingier when it comes to giving Zakah and different types of charity that bring one closer to Allah. Al-Mas`udi narrated from Salamah bin Kuhayl who reported from Abu Al-`Ubaydin that he asked Ibn Mas`ud about Al-Ma`un and he said, "It is what the people give to each other, like an axe, a pot, a bucket and similar items."

Hadith citations regarding the hypocrites

It was narrated from Ayyub, from Al-Hasan, from Abu Hurairah, that the Prophet said:

"Women who seek divorce and Khul' are like the female hypocrites." Al-Hasan said: "I did not hear it from anyone other than Abu Hurairah."

Grade : Sahih (Darussalam)

Reference   : Sunan an-Nasa'i 3461

Narrated Anas:

The Prophet said, "Love for the Ansar is a sign of faith and hatred for the Ansar is a sign of hypocrisy."

Reference   : Sahih al-Bukhari 17

Narrated Abu Hurairah:

that the Messenger of Allah said: "Two things will not be together in a hypocrite: Good manners, and Fiqh in the religion."

Grade : Da'if (Darussalam)

Reference   : Jami` at-Tirmidhi 2684

It was narrated that 'Ali said:

"The Prophet made a covenant with me that none would love me but a believer, and none would hate me but a hypocrite."

Grade : Sahih (Darussalam)

Reference   : Sunan an-Nasa'i 5022

It is narrated on the authority of Abdullah b. 'Amr that the Prophet observed:

"There are four characteristics, whoever has them all is a pure hypocrite, and whoever has one of its characteristics, he has one of the characteristics of hypocrisy, until he gives it up: When he speaks he lies, when he makes a covenant he betrays it, when he makes a promise he breaks it, and when he disputes he resorts to obscene speech." In the narration of Sufyan it is: "And if he has one of them, he has one of the characteristics of hypocrisy."

Reference   : Sahih Muslim 58

Narrated Ibn `Umar:

Allah's Messenger said, "A believer eats in one intestine (is satisfied with a little food), and a kafir (unbeliever) or a hypocrite eats in seven intestines (eats too much).

Reference   : Sahih al-Bukhari 5394

Narrated Abi Waih:

Hudhaifa bin Al-Yaman said, 'The hypocrites of today are worse than those of the lifetime of the Prophet, because in those days they used to do evil deeds secretly but today they do such deeds openly.'

Reference   : Sahih al-Bukhari 7113

Narrated Anas bin Malik:

The Prophet said, "Ad-Dajjal will come and encamp at a place close to Medina and then Medina will shake thrice whereupon every Kafir (disbeliever) and hypocrite will go out (of Medina) towards him."

Reference   : Sahih al-Bukhari 7124

Buraidah reported:

Messenger of Allah said, "That which differentiates us from the disbelievers and hypocrites is our performance of Salat. He who abandons it, becomes a disbeliever."

Reference   : Riyad us-Saliheen and At-Tirmidhi

It was narrated from Ibn 'Umar that :

The Messenger of Allah said: "The parable of the hypocrite is that of a sheep that hesitates between two flocks, sometimes following one, and sometimes following another, not knowing which to follow."

Grade : Sahih (Darussalam)

Reference   : Sunan an-Nasa'i 5037

It was narrated from Abu Hurairah that the Prophet said:

"Whoever dies without having fought or thought of fighting, he dies on one of the branches of hypocrisy."

Grade : Sahih (Darussalam)

Reference   : Sunan an-Nasa'i 3097

Narrated Buraydah ibn al-Hasib:

The Prophet said: Do not call a hypocrite sayyid (master), for if he is a sayyid, you will displease your Lord, Most High.

Grade : Sahih (Al-Albani)

Reference   : Sunan Abi Dawud 4977

Abu Hurairah reported

the Prophet said "He who dies without having fought or having felt fighting (against the infidels) to be his duty will die guilty of a kind of hypocrisy."

Grade : Sahih (Al-Albani)

Reference   : Sunan Abi Dawud 2502

It was narrated that 'Uthman said:

"The Messenger of Allah said: 'Whoever hears the Adhan when he is in the mosque, then goes out and does not go out for any (legitimate) need and does not intend to return, is a hypocrite.'"

Grade : Da'if (Darussalam)

Reference   : Sunan Ibn Majah 734

Abu Musa al-Ash'ari reported Allah's Messenger as saying:

A believer who recites the Qur'an is like an orange whose fragrance is sweet and whose taste is sweet; a believer who does not recite the Qur'an is like a date which has no fragrance but has a sweet taste; and the hypocrite who recites the Qur'an is like a basil whose fragrance is sweet, but whose taste is bitter; and a hypocrite who does not recite the Qur'an is like the colocynth which has no fragrance and has a bitter taste.

Reference   : Sahih Muslim 797 a

Narrated 'Abdullah bin 'Amr:

The Prophet said, "Whoever has the following four (characteristics) will be a pure hypocrite and whoever has one of the following four characteristics will have one characteristic of hypocrisy unless and until he gives it up.

1. Whenever he is entrusted, he betrays.

2. Whenever he speaks, he tells a lie.

3. Whenever he makes a covenant, he proves treacherous.

4. Whenever he quarrels, he behaves in a very imprudent, evil and insulting manner."

Reference   : Sahih al-Bukhari 34

Al-Mustawrid reported

the Prophet, said, "If anyone eats a meal at the expense of a Muslim's honour, Allah will feed him a like amount of Hellfire. If anyone clothes himself with a garment at the expense of a Muslim's honour, Allah will clothe him with a like amount of Hellfire. If anyone achieves a position of showing-off and hypocrisy at the expense of a Muslim's honour, Allah will put him in a position of showing-off and hypocrisy on the Day of Rising.

Grade : Sahih (Al-Albani)

Reference   : Al-Adab Al-Mufrad 240

Abu Huraira reported Allah's Messenger as saying:

The Similitude of a believer is that of (a standing) crop which the air continues to toss from one side to another; in the same way a believer always (receives the strokes) of misfortune. The similitude of a hypocrite is that of a cypress tree which does not move until it is uprooted.

Reference   : Sahih Muslim 2809 a

Ibn Abbas reported Allah's Messenger as saying:

If anyone wants to have his deeds widely publicised, Allah will publicise (his humiliation). And if anyone makes a hypocritical display (of his deeds) Allah will make a display of him.

Reference   : Sahih Muslim 2986

Abu Huraira reported: The Messenger of Allah , said,

"Verily, the first people to be judged on the Day of Resurrection will be a man who was martyred. He will be brought, the blessings of Allah will be made known and he will acknowledge them. Allah will say: What did you do about them? The man will say: I fought in your cause until I was martyred. Allah will say: You have lied, for you fought only that it would be said you were brave, and thus it was said. Then, Allah will order him to be dragged upon his face until he is cast into Hellfire. Another man studied religious knowledge, taught others, and recited the Quran. He will be

110

*brought, the blessings of Allah will be made known and he will
acknowledge them. Allah will say: What did you do about them?
The man will say: I learned religious knowledge, taught others,
and I recited the Quran for your sake. Allah will say: You have
lied, for you studied only that it would be said you are a scholar
and you recited the Quran only that it would be said you are a
reciter, and thus it was said. Then, Allah will order him to be
dragged upon his face until he is cast into Hellfire. Another man
was given an abundance of blessings from Allah and every kind of
wealth. He will be brought, the blessings of Allah will be made
known and he will acknowledge them. Allah will say: What did
you do about them? The man will say: I did not leave any good
cause beloved to you but that I spent on it for your sake. Allah will
say: You have lied, for you spent only that it would be said you are
generous, and thus it was said. Then, Allah will order him to be
dragged upon his face until he is cast into Hellfire."*

Reference   : Sahih Muslim 1905

Narrated Hudhaifa bin Al-Yaman:

*The people used to ask Allah's Messenger about the good but I
used to ask him about the evil lest I should be overtaken by them.
So I said, "O Allah's Messenger! We were living in ignorance and
in an (extremely) worst atmosphere, then Allah brought to us this
good (i.e., Islam); will there be any evil after this good?" He said,
"Yes." I said, 'Will there be any good after that evil?" He replied,
"Yes, but it will be tainted (not pure.)'' I asked, "What will be its
taint?" He replied, "(There will be) some people who will guide
others not according to my tradition? You will approve of some of
their deeds and disapprove of some others." I asked, "Will there be*

any evil after that good?" He replied, "Yes, (there will be) some people calling at the gates of the (Hell) Fire, and whoever will respond to their call, will be thrown by them into the (Hell) Fire." I said, "O Allah s Apostle! Will you describe them to us?" He said, "They will be from our own people and will speak our language." I said, "What do you order me to do if such a state should take place in my life?" He said, "Stick to the group of Muslims (Jamaah)and their Imam (ruler)." I said, "If there is neither a group of Muslims(Jamaah) nor an Imam (ruler)?" He said, "Then turn away from all those sects even if you were to bite (eat) the roots of a tree till death overtakes you while you are in that state."

Reference   :Sahih Bukhari 7084

Narrated Muhammad bin Zaid bin `Abdullah bin `Umar:

Some people said to Ibn `Umar, "When we enter upon our ruler(s) we say in their praise what is contrary to what we say when we leave them." Ibn `Umar said, "We used to consider this as hypocrisy."

Reference   : Sahih al-Bukhari 7178

Yahya related from Malik that he had heard that Said ibn al-Musayyab said,

"It is said that no-one except a hypocrite leaves the mosque after the call to prayer, except for someone who intends to return."

Reference   : Muwatta Imam Malik

Anas bin Malik narrated that :

Allah's Messenger said: "Whoever performs Salat for Allah for forty days in congregation, catching the first Takbir, two absolutions are written for him: absolution from the Fire, and absolution from the Fire, and absolution from hypocrisy."

Grade : Da'if (Darussalam)

Reference   : Jami` at-Tirmidhi 241

Ibn 'Umar and Abu Hurairah reported:

We heard the Messenger of Allah saying (while delivering Khutbah on his wooden pulpit), "Either some people (i.e., hypocrites) stop neglecting the Friday prayers, or Allah will seal their hearts and they will be among the heedless."

Reference   : Riyad us-Saliheen and Sahih Muslim

Buraidah said:

The Messenger of Allah said, "Do not address a hypocrite with the title of chief, (or similar titles of respect) for even if he deserves this title you will invite Allah's Wrath by using it for him."

Reference   Sunan Abi Dawood

It was narrated that Abu Hurairah said:

"The Messenger of Allah said: 'The most burdensome prayers for the hypocrites are the 'Isha' prayer and the Fajr prayer. If only they knew what (reward) there is in them, they would come to them even if they had to crawl.'"

Grade : Sahih (Darussalam)

Reference : Sunan Ibn Majah 797

It was narrated that 'Abdullah said:

"Whoever would like to meet Allah tomorrow (i.e. on the Day of Judgment) as a Muslim, let him preserve these five (daily) prayer when the call for them is given, for they are part of the ways of guidance, and Allah prescribed the ways of guidance to your Prophet. By Allah, if each of you prays in his house, you will have abandoned the Sunnah of your Prophet, and if you abandon the Sunnah of your Prophet you will go astray. I remember when no one stayed behind from the prayer except a hypocrite who was known for his hypocrisy. I have a man coming supported by two others, until he joined the row (of worshippers). There is no man who purifies himself and does it well, and comes to the mosque and prays there, but for every step that he takes, Allah raises him in status one degree thereby, and takes away one of his sins."

Grade : Hasan (Darussalam)

Reference : Sunan Ibn Majah 777

Narrated Abu Huraira:

Allah's Messenger said, "You see that the people are of different natures. Those who were the best in the pre-Islamic period, are also the best in Islam if they comprehend religious knowledge. You see that the best amongst the people in this respect (i.e. ambition of ruling) are those who hate it most. And you see that the worst among people is the double faced (person) who appears to these with one face and to the others with another face (i.e a hypocrite).

Reference : Sahih al-Bukhari 3493, 3494

Narrated Mu'adh ibn Anas:

The Prophet said: If anyone guards a believer from a hypocrite, Allah will send an angel who will guard his flesh on the Day of Resurrection from the fire of Jahannam; but if anyone attacks a Muslim saying something by which he wishes to disgrace him, he will be restrained by Allah on the bridge over Jahannam till he is acquitted of what he said.

Grade : Hasan (Al-Albani)

Reference   : Sunan Abi Dawud 4883

Salam ibn Miskin, quoting an old man who witnessed Abu Wa'il in a wedding feast, said:

They began to play, amuse and sing. He untied the support of his hand round his knees that were drawn up, and said: I heard Abdullah (ibn Mas'ud) say: I heard the apostle of Allah say: Singing produces hypocrisy in the heart.

Grade : Da'if (Al-Albani)

Reference   : Sunan Abi Dawud 4927

It is reported ʿAbdullāh bin Al-ʿAmr bin Al-ʿĀṣ said:

"Nifāq (hypocrisy) used to be something unusual amongst all the Īmān(faith). Soon, Īmān will be something strange amongst all the nifāq(hypocrisy)."

Ibn Baṭṭah, Al-Ibānah 1:173 article 6.

It is reported that Al-Ḥasan Al-Baṣrī said:

"Verily, you will find the believer (muʾmin) consistent time after time, upon one way, showing the same face; [whereas] you will find the hypocrite (munāfiq) changing colors, trying to be like everyone around him, running with every wind."

Abū Bakr Al-Daynūrī, Al-Mujālasah wa Jawāhir Al-ʿIlm #1936

It is reported that Al-Fuḍayl bin ʿAyyāḍ said:

"The believer speaks little and does alot, whereas the hypocrite (munāfiq) speaks a lot and does little. When the believer speaks, it is with wisdom, when he is silent, it is in deep thought, when he sees, he takes lessons, and when he acts, it is a cure. If this is the way you are, then you are in the constant worship [of your Lord.]"

Abū Nuʿaym, Ḥilyatu Al-Awliyāʾ 8:98.

It is reported that Al-Ḥasan Al-Baṣrī said:

"The believer does the best deeds yet is most fearful [that his deeds will not be accepted]. If he were to spend a mountain of wealth [in charity], he would not feel sure [of the reward] until he sees it. The more righteous and pious he becomes, the more he fears. But the hypocrite (munāfiq) says, 'There are so many people, I will be forgiven, no problem.' So he does wrong and evil deeds, yet holds foolish wishes about Allāh."

Al-Dhahabī, Siyar Aʿlām Al-Nubalāʾ 4:586.

It is reported that Al-Fuḍayl bin ʿAyyāḍ said:

"Verily, Allāh has angels who seek out the circles of remembrance [of Allāh], so be careful who you sit with; make sure it is not with an adherent of bidʿah, for Allāh does not look at them. And the sign of nifāq (hypocrisy in faith) is that a man mingles with an adherent of bidʿah."

Ibn Baṭṭah, Al-Ibānah Al-Kubrā 1:460

Signs of the Munafiq Compiled by Mindoro Islamic Research Center edited by Gregory Heary

1. WHEN HE SPEAKS HE LIES

2. WHEN HE MAKES A PROMISE HE BREAKS IT

3. WHEN YOU ENTRUST HIM WITH SOMETHING HE PROVES TREACHEROUS.

4. WHENEVER HE DISPUTES HE IS ABUSIVE

'Abdullah ibn 'Amr narrated that the Prophet said, "If anyone has four characteristics, he is a pure hypocrite, and if anyone has one of them, he has an aspect of hypocrisy until he gives it up: whenever he is trusted, he betrays his trust; whenever he speaks, he lies; when he makes an agreement, he breaks it; and when he quarrels, he deviates from the truth by speaking falsely." [al-Bukhari (34) and Muslim (58)]

5. HE LIKES TO SLANDER THE BELIEVERS

On the authority of 'Abdullah bin 'Amr bin Al-'As that the Prophet said: "A Muslim is the one from whose tongue and hands the Muslims are safe; and a Muhajir (Emigrant) is the one who refrains from what Allah has forbidden." [al-Bukhari (10) and Muslim (40)]

A munafiq is a tyrant, oppressor and bully.

Abu Hurairah reported: The Prophet said, "By Allah, he is not a believer! By Allah, he is not a believer! By Allah, he is not a believer." It was asked, "Who is that, O Messenger of Allah?" He said, "One whose neighbour does not feel safe from his evil." [al-Bukhari (6016) and Muslim (46)] Another narration of Muslim is: Messenger of Allah said, "He will not enter Jannah whose neighbour is not secure from his wrongful conduct".

6. HE STARTS FITNAH AMONG THE BELIEVERS AND THEN HE PRETENDS HE DOESN'T KNOW WHO STARTED IT

7. THEY ARE TIGHT FISTED AND STINGY

And nothing prevents their contributions from being accepted from them except that they disbelieved in Allah and in His Messenger (Muhammad); and that they came not to As-Salat (the prayer) except in a lazy state; and that they offer not contributions but unwillingly. (At-Tawbah 9:54)

8. HE IS A COWARD AND PUTS DODGY CONDITIONS ON JIHAD

Those who believe say: "Why is not a Surah (chapter of the Qur'an) sent down (for us)? But when a decisive Surah (explaining and ordering things) is sent down, and fighting (Jihad ¬ holy fighting in Allah's Cause) is mentioned (i.e. ordained) therein, you will see those in whose hearts is a disease (of hypocrisy) looking at you with a look of one fainting to death. But it was better for them (hypocrites, to listen to Allah and to obey Him). (Muhammad 47:20)

9. THEY ARE LAZY IN IBAADAH

And nothing prevents their contributions from being accepted from them except that they disbelieved in Allah and in His Messenger (Muhammad); and that they came not to As-Salat (the prayer) except in a lazy state; and that they offer not contributions but unwillingly. (At-Tawbah 9:54)

Abu Huraira narrated that the Messenger of Allah said "The heaviest salat for the hypocrite is that of Isha'a and Fajr and if they knew what was in them they would have attended them even if it meant crawling, and I have a strong desire to order the salat to be established, then order a man to lead the people in salat then I would go with some men carrying bundles of wood to a people not attending the salat and burn their houses on them." [al-Bukhari (657) and Muslim (651)]

10. WHEN THERE IS A VALID JIHAD HE CHEERS FOR THE DISBELIEVERS AGAINST THE MUJAHIDEEN

If good befalls you, it grieves them, but if a calamity overtakes you, they say: "We took our precaution beforehand," and they turn away rejoicing. (At-Tawbah 9:50)

11. THEY LIKE TO ASK QUESTIONS ONLY ALLAH CAN ANSWER

Ja'far Ibn Abdullah narrated: We were with Malik Ibn Anas when a man came to him and said: "O Abu Abdullah (Allah said) 'Ar-Rahman upon the Throne Istawa' (20:5), how was His Istiwa? Imam Malik inclined his head and was silent until the sweat of fever covered his brow, then he looked up and said: "Istiwa is not unknown, the Kayf (how) is uncomprehendable, believing in it is wajib (obligatory), and asking about it is bid'ah (innovation), and I do not think that you are anything but an innovator." Then he ordered that the man be expelled. [Abu-Naeem Al-Asbahani in 'Hilyatul-Awliya wa Tabaqat Al-Asfiya' (Vol. 6, pg. 325-326)]

12) HE CAN'T RETAIN KNOWLEDGE

And among them are some who listen to you (O Muhammad) till, when they go out from you, they say to those who have received knowledge: "What has he said just now? Such are men whose hearts Allah has sealed, and they follow their lusts (evil desires). (Muhammad 47:16)

Abu Huraira reported that Allah's Messenger said: "Two characterstics cannot combine in a hypocrite: good character and an understanding of religion." [Sunan Tirmidhi (5/49) No. 2684, al-Thiqat Ibn Hibban (8/227) No. 13149, al-Mu'jam al-Awsat al-Tabarani (8/75) No. 8010, al-Madkhal ila al-Sunan al-Kubra al-Bayhaqi (pg. 256) No. 357]

Narrated Muawiya: I heard the Prophet saying, "If Allah wants to do good to a person, He makes him comprehend the religion. I am just a distributor, but the grant is from Allah. (And remember) that this nation (Muslims) will keep on following Allah's teachings strictly and they will not be harmed by any one going on a different path till Allah's order (Day of Judgment) is established." [al-Bukhari (71) and Muslim (1037)]

Narrated By Abu Huraira: Some people asked the Prophet: "Who is the most honorable amongst the people?" He replied, "The most honorable among them is the one who is the most Allah-fearing." They said, "O Allah's Prophet! We do not ask about this." He said, "Then the most honorable person is Joseph, Allah's Prophet, the son of Allah's Prophet, the son of Allah's Prophet, the son of Allah's Khalil." They said, "We do not ask about this." He said, "Then you want to ask me about the Arabs' descent?" They said, "Yes." He said, "Those who were best in the pre-lslamic period, are the best in Islam, if they comprehend (the religious knowledge)." [Sahih Bukhari, Vol 4, Book 55, Hadith 593]

13. HE LIKES TO HIGHLIGHT THE NEGATIVE ASPECTS OF ISLAMIC HISTORY

14) HE GOES TO THE FRONTLINE FOR BOOTY OR MUTINY

Had they marched out with you, they would have added to you nothing except disorder, and they would have hurried about in your midst (spreading corruption) and sowing sedition among you, and there are some among you who would have listened to them. And Allah is the All-Knower of the Zalimun (polytheists and wrong-doers, etc.). (At-Tawbah 9:47)

15. HE PAYS ATTENTION TO FANCY DRESS AND FLOWERED SPEECH AND FORGETS TO PURIFY HIS HEART

And when you look at them, their bodies please you; and when they speak, you listen to their words. They are as blocks of wood propped up. They think that every cry is against them. They are the enemies, so beware of them. May Allah curse them! How are they denying (or deviating from) the Right Path. (Al-Munafiqun 63:4)

They have a eloquent tongue.

Narrated Ibn 'Umar: 'Two men came from the East and addressed the people who wondered at their eloquent speeches. On that the Messenger of Allah said: "Some eloquent speech is as effective as magic."' [Sahih Bukhari (7/19) No. 5146]

Abu Dhar said, "I was with the Prophet one day and I heard him saying: "There is something I fear for my Ummah than the Dajjal." It was then that I became afraid, so I said: "Oh Rasool Allah! Which thing is that?" He said; "Misguided and astray scholars." [Musnad Ahmad (5/145) No. 21334 and 21335]

16. HE IS REBELLIOUS TO QUR'AN AND SUNNAH

But no, by your Lord, they can have no Faith, until they make you (O Muhammad) judge in all disputes between them, and find in themselves no resistance against your decisions, and accept (them) with full submission. (4:65)

17. HE LIKES TO TAKE HIS DISPUTES TO THE KAFIR COURTHOUSE

Have you seen those (hyprocrites) who claim that they believe in that which has been sent down to you, and that which was sent down before you, and they wish to go for judgement (in their disputes) to the Taghut (false judges, etc.) while they have been ordered to reject them. But Shaitan (Satan) wishes to lead them far astray. (4:60)

While 'Allama al-Shinqiti- has said: To commit shirk with Allah in judging is of the same meaning as to commit shirk in His worship, there is no difference between the two in any manner. There is no difference in any sense between he who follows a system (nizam) other than Allah's system or law other than Allah's law (sharia) and he who worships an idol or prostrates to a false god. They are the same and both are polytheists [associating others] with Allah. [Adwa' al-Bayan, (7/162)]

18. THEY HAVE TWO FACES AND TWO TONGUES

And when it is said to them (hypocrites) : "Believe as the people (followers of Muhammad, Al-Ansar and Al-Muhajirun) have believed," they say: "Shall we believe as the fools have believed?" Verily, they are the fools, but they know not. (Al-Baqarah 2:13)

And when they meet those who believe, they say: "We believe," but when they are alone with their Shayatin (devils

- polytheists, hypocrites, etc.), they say: "Truly, we are with you; verily, we were but mocking." (Al-Baqarah 2:14)

Allah mocks at them and gives them increase in their wrong-doings to wander blindly. (Al-Baqarah 2:15)

19. HE LIKES TO CALL THE MUSLIMS FOOL

And when it is said to them (hypocrites) : "Believe as the people (followers of Muhammad Peace be upon him , Al-Ansar and Al-Muhajirun) have believed," they say: "Shall we believe as the fools have believed?" Verily, they are the fools, but they know not. (Al-Baqarah 2:13)

20. THEY LIKE TO SIT IN PLACES WHERE ALLAH'S DEEN IS RIDICULED

And it has already been revealed to you in the Book (this Qur'an) that when you hear the Verses of Allah being denied and mocked at, then sit not with them, until they engage in a talk other than that; (but if you stayed with them) certainly in that case you would be like them. Surely, Allah will collect the hypocrites and disbelievers all together in Hell, (An-Nisa 4:140)

Allah promised to dump them in the Hellfire for such a crime and Allah mentioned the hypocrites in the Ayah because they gravitate towards such things.

21. THEY CANNOT PRACTISE AL WALAA WAL BARAA

They have the greatest enemies of Islam for their friends and feel comfortable in their company.

Allah tells you in Surah 60:1 that you should not take His enemies and your enemies as your friends.

O you who believe! Take not My enemies and your enemies (i.e. disbelievers and polytheists, etc.) as friends, showing affection towards them, while they have disbelieved in what has come to you of the truth (i.e. Islamic Monotheism, this Qur'an, and Muhammad), and have driven out the Messenger (Muhammad) and yourselves (from your homeland) because you believe in Allah your Lord! If you have come forth to strive in My Cause and to seek My Good Pleasure, (then take not these disbelievers and polytheists, etc., as your friends). You show friendship to them in secret, while I am All-Aware of what you conceal and what you reveal. And whosoever of you (Muslims) does that, then indeed he has gone (far) astray, (away) from the Straight Path. (Al-Mumtahinah 60:1)

You will not find any people who believe in Allah and the Last Day, making friendship with those who oppose Allah and His Messenger (Muhammad), even though they were their fathers, or their sons, or their brothers, or their kindred (people). For such He has written Faith in their hearts, and strengthened them with Ruh (proofs, light and true guidance) from Himself. And We will admit them to Gardens (Paradise) under which rivers flow, to dwell therein (forever). Allah is pleased with them, and they with Him.

They are the Party of Allah. Verily, it is the Party of Allah that will be the successful. (Al-Mujadilah 58:22)

22. THEY INSULT ALLAH AND HIS RASUL

They have no love for Allah and His Rasul and insult them.

If you ask them (about this), they declare: "We were only talking idly and joking." Say: "Was it at Allah, and His Ayat (proofs, evidences, verses, lessons, signs, revelations, etc.) and His Messenger that you were mocking?" (9:65)

Make no excuse; you have disbelieved after you had believed. If We pardon some of you, We will punish others amongst you because they were Mujrimun (disbelievers, polytheists, sinners, criminals, etc.). (At-Tawbah 9:66)

23. THEY SPEAK ABOUT ISLAM SARCASTICALLY

And whenever there comes down a Surah (chapter from the Qur'an), some of them (hypocrites) say: "Which of you has had his Faith increased by it?" As for those who believe, it has increased their Faith, and they rejoice. (At-Tawbah 9:124)

24. THEY BELIEVE THAT ALLAH PROMISES THEM FAKE PROMISES

And when the hypocrites and those in whose hearts is a disease (of doubts) said: "Allah and His Messenger promised us nothing but delusions!" (Al-Ahzab 33:12)

25. THEY DESPAIR QUITE EASILY AND THEY HAVE NO TAWAKKAL

Those (i.e. believers) unto whom the people (hypocrites) said, "Verily, the people (pagans) have gathered against you (a great army), therefore, fear them." But it (only) increased them in Faith, and they said: "Allah (Alone) is Sufficient for us, and He is the Best Disposer of affairs (for us)." (3:173)

"O my sons! Go you and enquire about Yusuf (Joseph) and his brother, and never give up hope of Allah's Mercy. Certainly no one despairs of Allah's Mercy, except the people who disbelieve." (Yusuf 12:87)

26. THEY SPREAD CORRUPTION IN THE LAND AND PRETEND TO BE PEACEFUL

And when it is said to them: "Make not mischief on the earth," they say: "We are only peacemakers." (2:11)

Verily! They are the ones who make mischief, but they perceive not. (Al-Baqarah 2:12)

27. THEY ENJOIN EVIL AND FORBID GOOD

The hypocrites, men and women, are from one another, they enjoin (on the people) Al-Munkar (i.e. disbelief and polytheism of all kinds and all that Islam has forbidden), and forbid (people) from Al-Ma'ruf (i.e. Islamic Monotheism and all that Islam orders one to do), and they close their hands [from giving (spending in Allah's Cause) alms, etc.]. They have forgotten Allah, so He has forgotten them. Verily, the hypocrites are the Fasiqun (rebellious, disobedient to Allah). (At-Tawbah 9:67)

28. THEY ARE GREEDY FOR DUNYA AND THEY ARGUE ABOUT IT

Narrated Abu Saeed al-Khudri: 'Ali bin Abi Talib sent a piece of gold not yet taken out of its ore, in a tanned leather container to Allah's Messenger. The Messenger of Allah distributed that amongst four Persons: 'Uyaina bin Badr, Aqra' bin Habis, Zaid al-Khail and the fourth was either Alqama or Amir bin at-Tufail. On that, one of his companions said, "We are more deserving of this (gold) than these (persons)."

When that news reached the Prophet, he said, "Don't you trust me though I am a trustee of the One in the Heavens, and I receive the news of Heaven (i.e. Divine Inspiration) both in the morning and in the evening?" There got up a man with sunken eyes, raised cheek bones, raised forehead, a thick beard, a shaven head and a waist sheet that was tucked up and he said, "O Messenger of Allah, fear Allah!"

The Prophet said, "Woe to you! Am I not of all the people of the earth the most entitled to fear Allah?" Then that man went away. Khalid bin al-Walid said, "O Messenger of Allah! Shall I chop his neck off?" The Prophet said, "No, for he may offer prayers." Khalid said, "Numerous are those who offer prayers and say by their tongues (i.e. mouths) what is not in their hearts."

Allah's Messenger said, "I have not been ordered (by Allah) to search the hearts of the people or cut open their bellies." Then the Prophet looked at him (i.e. that man) while the latter was going away and said, "From the offspring of this (man there will come out (people) who will recite the Qur'an continuously and elegantly but it will not exceed their throats.

(They will neither understand it nor act upon it). They would go out of the religion (i.e. Islam) as an arrow goes through a game's body." I think he also said, "If I should be present at their time I would kill them as the nations a Thamud were killed." [al-Bukhari (4351) and Muslim (1064)]

29. THEY ALWAYS THINK THE WORST ABOUT ALLAH

And that He may punish the Munafiqun (hypocrites), men and women, and also the Mushrikun men and women, who think evil thoughts about Allah, for them is a disgraceful torment, and the Anger of Allah is upon them, and He has cursed them and prepared Hell for them, and worst indeed is that destination. (Al-Fath 48:6)

30. THEY ALWAYS ESTABLISH MASJID DIRAAR

And as for those who put up a mosque by way of harming and disbelief, and to disunite the believers, and as an outpost for those who warred against Allah and His Messenger (Muhammad) aforetime, they will indeed swear that their intention is nothing but good. Allah bears witness that they are certainly liars. (At-Tawbah 9:107)

31. THEY USE IBADAAT LIKE HAJJ, SALAH TO DECEIVE THE MUSLIMS AND GAIN RESPECT

Narrated By Abu Said: I heard the Prophet saying, "Allah will bring forth the severest Hour, and then all the Believers, men and women, will prostrate themselves before Him, but there will remain those who used to prostrate in the world for showing off and for gaining good reputation. Such people will try to prostrate (on the Day of Judgment) but their back swill be as stiff as if it is one bone (a single vertebra)." [Sahih Bukhari, Vol 6, Book 60, Hadith #441]

32. EVERY TIME THE HYPOCRITE OPENS HIS MOUTH TO SPEAK, HE EXPOSES HIMSELF

Even though the Munafiq might think he is clever and thinks he can deceive the believers, he still exposes himself.

Allah reminds us in the Quran that the Munafiq can be recognized by their speech. Nay not just their speech but the very tone of their speech even on the rare occasions they speak good or remain silent.

Had We willed, We could have shown them to you, and you should have known them by their marks, but surely, you will know them by the tone of their speech! And Allah knows all your deeds. (Muhammad 47:30)

33. THE MUNAFIQ LIKES TO BE PRAISED FOR THINGS HE DOES NOT DO

Think not that those who rejoice in what they have done (or brought about), and love to be praised for what they have not done,- think not you that they are rescued from the torment, and for them is a painful torment. (3:188)

34. THE MUNAFIQ DOES NOT GIVE THE CORRECT TAFSEER OF THE AYAH, INSTEAD HE PUTS HIS OWN SPIN ON IT

And when you see those who engage in a false conversation about Our Verses (of the Qur'an) by mocking at them, stay away from them till they turn to another topic. And if Shaitan (Satan) causes you to forget, then after the remembrance sit not you in the company of those people who are the Zalimun (polytheists and wrongdoers, etc.). (Al-An'am 6:68)

The Munafiq will put his own spin on the Ayah to lead astray unsuspecting Muslims. The false conversations Allah speaks about in the above Ayah, is the spin the Munafiq puts on the Quranic Ayahs.

Abu Dhar said, "I was with the Prophet (SAW) one day and I heard him saying: "There is something I fear for my Ummah than the Dajjal." It was then that I became afraid, so I said: "Oh Rasool Allah! Which thing is that?" He said; "Misguided and astray scholars." [Musnad Ahmad (5/145) No. 21334 and 21335]

35. MUNAFIQS LIKE TO QUOTE FABRICATED HADITH

Example of a fabricated hadith:

"We have come back from the minor jihad to the major one" someone asked: "What is the major Jihad O Messenger of Allah?" he replied: "Jihad of the nafs," (This report, collected

131

by Bayhaqi is fabricated as mentioned in Mannaar as-Subl of Ibn Qayyim al-Jawziyyah)

Ibn Taymiyyah said: "This Hadith has no sources and nobody whomsoever in the field of Islamic knowledge has narrated it. Jihad against the disbelievers is the most noble of actions and moreover it is the most important action for mankind." [al-Furqan (pg. 56)]

On the authority of Abu Sa'id al-Khudri (RA): the Messenger of Allah (SAW) said, "The best type of Jihad is speaking a true word in the presence of a tyrant ruler." [Sunan Abu Dawud (4/124) No. 4344, Sunan Ibn Majah (5/144) No. 4011, Sunan Tirmidhi (4/471) No. 2174]

Do you consider the providing of drinking water to the pilgrims and the maintenance of Al-Masjid-al-Haram (at Makkah) as equal to the worth of those who believe in Allah and the Last Day, and strive hard and fight in the Cause of Allah? They are not equal before Allah. And Allah guides not those people who are the Zalimun (polytheists and wrong-doers). (At-Tawbah 9:19)

This fabricated hadith also contradicts a Sahih Hadith which is in Abu Dawood above.

36. THE MUNAFIQ IS HARSHLY ARGUMENTATIVE

They are adamant in hanging on to their false beliefs even though you provide them with clear verses contradicting their falsehood.

Al-Hafiz Abu Ishaq Ibrahim bin 'Abdur-Rahman bin Ibrahim bin Duhaym recorded that Damrah narrated that two men took their dispute to the Prophet, and he gave a judgment to the benefit of whoever among them had the right. The person who lost the dispute said, "I do not agree." The other person asked him, "What do you want then" He said, "Let us go to Abu Bakr As-Siddiq." They went to Abu Bakr and the person who won the dispute said, "We went to the Prophet with our dispute and he issued a decision in my favor." Abu Bakr said, "Then the decision is that which the Messenger of Allah issued." The person who lost the dispute still rejected the decision and said, "Let us go to 'Umar bin Al-Khattab." When they went to 'Umar, the person who won the dispute said, "We took our dispute to the Prophet and he decided in my favor, but this man refused to submit to the decision."

'Umar bin Al-Khattab asked the second man and he concurred. 'Umar went to his house and emerged from it holding aloft his sword. He struck the head of the man who rejected the Prophet's decision with the sword and killed him. Consequently, Allah revealed, (But no, by your Lord, they can have no Faith, until they make you judge in all disputes between them... (An-Nisa 4:65)). [Tafseer Ibn Katheer (2/351-352)]

O Prophet (Muhammad)! Strive hard against the disbelievers and the hypocrites, and be harsh against them, their abode is Hell, - and worst indeed is that destination. (At-Tawbah 9:73)

37. THE MUNAFIQ THINKS EVERY CRY IS AGAINST THEM

And when you look at them, their bodies please you; and when they speak, you listen to their words. They are as blocks of wood propped up. They think that every cry is against them. They are the enemies, so beware of them. May Allah curse them! How are they denying (or deviating from) the Right Path. (Al-Munafiqun 63:4)

38. THE MUNAFIQ USES HIS ISLAM AND SEEKS KNOWLEDGE TO ATTAIN FAME AND FORTUNE

Ka'b ibn Malik (RA) reported that he heard Allah's Messenger (SAW) say: "If anyone seeks knowledge in order to compete with the scholars or to concur with the foolish or to direct the faces of the people toward himself, Allah will put him in the fire." [Sunan Tirmidhi (5/32) No. 2654, Sunan Darimi (1/374) No. 379, Sunan Ibn Majah (1/170) No. 254, Mustadrak al-Haakim (1/161) No. 293, Sahih Ibn Hibban (1/278) No. 77, Shu'ab al-Iman al-Bayhaqi (3/269) No. 1636, al-Mu'jam al-Awsat al-Tabarani (6/32) No. 5708]

39. THE MUNAFIQ LIES ON HIS HEALTH

They claim they cannot fast in Ramadan.

They claim they cannot go to Hajj.

They claim they could not make it to Jumu'ah.

40. THE MUNAFIQ DOES NOT FREQUENT THE MASJID

41. THE MUNAFIQ USES THE EXCUSE OF THEIR FAMILY AND THEIR WEALTH TO ABANDON JIHAD

Those of the bedouins who lagged behind will say to you: "Our possessions and our families occupied us, so ask forgiveness for us." They say with their tongues what is not in their hearts. Say: "Who then has any power at all (to intervene) on your behalf with Allah, if He intends you hurt or intends you benefit? Nay, but Allah is Ever All-Aware of what you do. (Al-Fath 48:11)

42. THE MUNAFIQ DOES NOT REMEMBER ALLAH AND DOES NOT DO DHIKR

They forget Allah, so Allah forgets about them.

The hypocrites, men and women, are from one another, they enjoin (on the people) Al-Munkar (i.e. disbelief and polytheism of all kinds and all that Islam has forbidden), and forbid (people) from Al-Ma'ruf (i.e. Islamic Monotheism and all that Islam orders one to do), and they close their hands [from giving (spending in Allah's Cause) alms, etc.]. They have forgotten Allah, so He has forgotten them. Verily, the hypocrites are the Fasiqun (rebellious, disobedient to Allah). (At-Tawbah 9:67)

Abu Huraira (RA) reported that Allah's Messenger (SAW) said, "The world, with all that it contains, is accursed except for dhikr (the remembrance of Allah) that which pleases Allah; and the religious scholars and seekers of knowledge." [Sunan Tirmidhi (4/561) 2322 and Sunan Ibn Majah (5/231)

4112, (Abu Eesa al-Tirmidhi said: this hadeeth is hasan ghareeb)]

And whosoever turns away (blinds himself) from the remembrance of the Most Beneficent (Allah) (i.e. this Qur'an and worship of Allah), We appoint for him Shaitan (Satan devil) to be a Qarin (an intimate companion) to him. (Az-Zukhruf 43:36)

43. THE MUNAFIQ MAKES FAKE PROMISES TO HIS FRIENDS AND COLLEAGUES

Have you not observed the hypocrites who say to their friends among the people of the Scripture who disbelieve: "(By Allah) If you are expelled, we (too) indeed will go out with you, and we shall never obey any one against you, and if you are attacked (in fight), we shall indeed help you." But Allah is Witness, that they verily, are liars. (Al-Hashr 59:11)

Surely, if they (the Jews) are expelled, never will they (hypocrites) go out with them, and if they are attacked, they will never help them. And if they do help them, they (hypocrites) will turn their backs, so they will not be victorious. (Al-Hashr 59:12)

44. THE MUNAFIQ IS FILLED WITH PRIDE, ARROGANCE AND HAUGHTINESS

45. THE MUNAFIQ DOES NOT CONSIDER ALL THE NON-MUSLIMS TO BE KUFFAR (DISBELIEVERS)

www.ingramcontent.com/pod-product-compliance
Lightning Source LLC
Chambersburg PA
CBHW061651120626
46550CB00003B/907